Roger Mason was born at Skipton, Yorkshire in 1940. He was educated at Giggleswick School and Queen's College, Oxford where he read law. After qualifying as a barrister his interest in architecture and local history led him to become a town planner. He now lives in a village in Oxfordshire and teaches town planning at Oxford Polytechnic.

Also by Roger Mason:

GRANNY'S VILLAGE

ROGER MASON

Plain Tales from Yorkshire

Futura
Macdonald & Co
London & Sydney

A Futura Book

First published in Great Britain in 1982 by
Macdonald & Co (Publishers) Ltd
London & Sydney

First Futura edition 1983

Copyright © 1982 by Roger Mason

ISBN 0 7088 2359 9

Filmset, printed and bound in Great Britain by
Hazell Watson & Viney Ltd, Aylesbury, Bucks

Futura Publications
A Division of
Macdonald & Co (Publishers) Ltd
Maxwell House
74 Worship Street
London EC2A 2EN

Contents

To seven brave Yorkshire characters
who trusted their tales to me:

MIRIAM PARKINSON
JACK CARL
KIT CALVERT
ELSIE WILKINSON
LAWRIE MURFIELD
BERT HALEY
JENNIE PORTER

Acknowledgements

Illustrations
The author and publishers wish to thank the people about whom the author has written in this book for allowing them to use a number of family photographs.

In researching a book of this kind the writer meets hundreds of people and is given all varieties of help. It is not really practicable to thank them all, but I hope they will understand that they are not forgotten if their name is not mentioned.

I owe a great deal to the help of BBC local radio stations and their staff for suggesting possible subjects, and particularly:
Peter Hawkins of Radio Leeds,
Gillian Hush of the BBC's Manchester Studio,
Graham Henderson of Radio Humberside,
Ralph Robinson of Radio Sheffield and
Graeme Aldous of Radio Cleveland.

In Sheffield I was given a very warm welcome and every help by the staff of Joseph Elliot & Sons Limited who manufacture the most excellent traditional cutlery. Mr Roe and Mr Revitt among the directors, the office staff, and all the craftsmen, particularly Harry Drabble the hand-forger, made my wife and I, but especially my daughter Anna, feel very much at home in a cutlery factory.

In Whitby I owe thanks to Eric Thomson, the honorary curator of the Lifeboat Museum. On Humberside I had a great deal of help from Jim Thompson and Brian Roustoby, respectively a sailing-master and archivist of the Humber Keel and Sloop Preservation Society. Mr Feather, curator of the Industrial Museum, Bradford, proved generous with his help.
I must also thank David and Edna Price for their early advice.

Above all I am grateful to my parents, Stanley and Dorothy Mason, not only for raising me as a Yorkshireman, but also for looking after me, advising and refreshing me with steak pie and brandy, during my many flying research visits to the north. And what shall I say about my wife, Margaret, who has acted as unpaid chauffeur, photographer's assistant and art director, not to mention soothing the wearied brow of the author of this deathless prose? Why, I suppose I shall have to give her a kiss and say nowt.

A Yorkshire Handful

A scarlet-coated militiaman stood at the top of Brook Street one sunny morning in August 1914. Raising his bugle to his lips he played a call to arms, summoning the whole of Cleckheaton to war. All the lads gathered excitedly round this splendid figure of a Yorkshire volunteer. It was a grand sight and a moment from history. Sensing his newly found importance the bugler lingered triumphantly on the final notes, snapped his burnished instrument smartly down and prepared to march to glory. But muck is never far from brass in Yorkshire and the assembled lads were already sniffing ostentatiously, grubby fingers to noses. They knew him, the man beneath the fine uniform. He was a wiredrawer, and you could always tell a wiredrawer by his smell.

Those simple bugle notes, repeated everywhere throughout the county, signalled a change that would always divide the lives of those who grew up before the Great War to End Wars from those who came after. It was not just because of the heavy toll of lives, the fathers, husbands, sons, who never returned. Though, if you step into any county church or, better still, enter Beverley Minster on a winter's day, and stand in cold silence before the memorials, then you will see list after list of names, local names of local families. 'Men of the East Yorkshire Regiment killed in France.' There are many times the number who died in the Second World War.

No, it is not simply the war and the dead, for other changes came with them which shook the foundations of that stable world. Their time is gone and we learn of it as dry history. But the survivors are still with us, able to make it live again through their tales. They preserve the values, beliefs, and above all, the precious memories of their distant childhood.

Seven tales are recorded here, the memories of people from widely different backgrounds but all within the old County of Yorkshire. They are strong characters endued with self-respect and a sense of humour. As far as possible they have been left to speak in their own words.

Miriam Parkinson is the daughter of a market-gardener from the Vale of York, a lover still of the quiet, arable countryside where she was born. Jack Carl grew up in smoky Sheffield, to the clang of hammer on steel and the sparks from grinding-wheels. He revels in his grinder's skills, in tales of old cutlers and in his mates' drinking feats at the pub. Kit Calvert, a dalesman, once a farmer, still keeps his pony and trap for journeys in Wensleydale. Elsie Wilkinson gladly obeyed a stern Victorian mother until her dying day, worked long hours at the loom, and then married as she wished. Lawrie Murfield has lived all his life as a fisherman in Whitby and believes there is no greater career, except, perhaps to be coxswain of the Whitby lifeboat. Bert Haley lived through war and the dole queue in Cleckheaton and survived as a natural philosopher and first class engine-tenter. Jenny Porter, the longest lived of them all, had a rough life as mate of a sailing barge, and is still fit, active and cheerful, with a positively alarming memory for the past.

Take their stories separately, and each has its own pattern and personality, fascinating to follow. But like the distinct, pungent brews that are blended into a strong, smooth old whiskey, they work with each other to tell us something more. Bottled and matured, these plain tales bring us the essence of the old County of Yorkshire in its great days since the turn of the century.

The scarlet-coated wiredrawer has marched away to die for his King and Country. Bert Haley remembers him as he stood, proudly, in the sunlight, to celebrate his brief moment of glory. We have the good fortune to share this memory.

Miriam Parkinson
and the Vale of York

Hold out your right hand in front of you, palm up. Imagine your fingers are rivers, running down from the hills, as they do from the Pennines. There are more rivers than fingers, of course, from the Swale in the northernmost of the Dales, to the Sheaf at Sheffield. On the eastern side of your hand the thumb represents the river Derwent, flowing down from the North York Moors to join the Ouse. Then the Vale of York is cupped in your hand, its historic capital, the City of York, placed centrally where roads and rivers meet, and where ships could sail upriver to market.

The Vale is a rich land, built up of soil brought down from the hills, and always vulnerable to floods. This is particularly true of the low-lying, southern part of the Vale, the land around Selby, where the sluggish Ouse winds its embanked way down to the Humber. Only fifteen miles south of York, and a couple of miles from Selby, Miriam Parkinson was born in the small agricultural village of Hemingbrough in April 1897.

Living Right Grand

She was out, escaped, swinging contentedly on the five barred gate by the tool shed. A bonny lass, little Miriam Parkinson, nearly four years old, watching the soft snow crumble in the lines of bootmarks that marched down the village street, and waiting for her Dada. He would be among the last to come out of church, for he rang the bells in the tall, stone spire that pointed to God. A spire that kept watch for miles over the flat meadows where she walked in summer. Sometimes Dada went to Selby Abbey to ring second bell in a peel and then he was very late. But Miriam would always wait for Dada, and he called her 'my honey' when he came. She wanted to be Dada's honey always.

Church was over at last. There were the ladies coming out of church, black figures against a wide white landscape, making more bootmarks in the snow. Miriam barely noticed them, it was all so usual. Her home was just along Finkle Street and from the gate she could see the swinging umbrellas, prayer books clasped in one gloved hand, and the other employed in keeping up long skirts out of the wet. But for some reason all the ladies, every one of them, also had a handkerchief clutched with the prayer book, and every now and then it was dabbed to the eyes. She could hear the buzz of interested talk as each group passed by. The bell was still tolling. Why? Dada would never be home at this rate. Then Uncle John came down the street, hands in his pockets.

Just as he stood waiting for Miriam to swing the gate open Mama came out of the kitchen. She was wearing her best, black, silk dress with a white apron and the cooking cuffs she still kept from her working years at the Talbot Hotel. She looked at Uncle John inquiringly, but he never spoke, being a man of few words. Mama stood, listening to the single bell tolling, then she said, 'John, is that for the Queen?' He just nodded. Mama took out her handkerchief and went back into the kitchen.

The street was quiet again, except for a small group of labouring men gathered at the end of Finkle Street, by the Half Moon. Miriam swung the gate again, wondering what it was all about, until she felt a soft touch by her side. It was Kruger, their bronze retriever, mouth open and laughing with misty breath as if to say, 'I'm off duty, aren't I, but still waiting for the master.' So they stood patiently together until the bells ceased tolling. There he was at last, a Gladstonian figure, black-coated, well-whiskered under the chin, with bushy eyebrows, and those lovely moustaches a daughter could stroke and pull a little if he teased her, his hair well oiled for Sunday. Dada was home ·and now Mama could serve Sunday dinner over her handkerchief.

Queen Victoria's death proved matter for serious concern, for it seemed like the end of an established world. Miriam could only listen and wonder. She was not allowed to talk. Although the doors were shut on the snow that January in 1901, and their own church was momentarily silent, they could still hear the bells of Selby Abbey ringing across the Ouse. In the flat landscape of the Vale of York their village of Hemingbrough lay hidden among trees in the heart of its fields, revealed to the passer-by on the main road only by its church spire. The houses were old, brownish-red brick, like Miriam's own, with their clay-tiled roofs to match, and the working countryside started at every door – closes, paddocks, the lanes to the arable fields, or water-meadows beside the Ouse. There was a landing place by the river, half a mile from the village, where children could sit to watch the sailing barges, with their brown or white sails, going down river to Hull and the sea, or up to York.

Miriam lived in the Old Vicarage, in the happiness of a full and contented family existence. Her father, George Parkinson, was a market gardener, and all the business of his life, the beasts, gear, fruit, work, the very land itself, flowed round her home, a province of wonders. Four acres of garden land where her father bent his back, a pasture beyond, with Mrs Lee's cow, Molly, and then their own goats. Close round the house stood an orchard with two pear trees, apples in many varieties, Keswicks, Ladyfingers, Balsams, Russets, and green Burnots for pies, big as a saucer. At the side, by the hedge, was one tree that neighbours were always telling Dada to grub up and then he always laughed, shook his head and pulled his beard. 'It's grand for eggs,' he would say. Miriam remembered buckets full of the manky, Cockpit apples, full of maggots, waiting their turn to stew over the kitchen range, in a cauldron hanging on a reckonhook, to make a savoury mash for the scratching hens.

In snowy January most of the work went on inside, unless Dada had a fine day for digging the vegetable beds. He spent a lot of time digging. In bad weather there were apples to be turned over in the granary loft, teased out of the straw, the bad ones given to the hens, the good ones carefully returned to their beds to the sound of regular sneezing because of the dusty air. The new piglet in its sty would get a good scrubbing, to keep it clean, healthy and happy, whilst its predecessor's joints swung from hooks in the larder across the back yard. Every morning the leafless branches of the bower of lilac and laburnum, which led from back door to privy, dripped on the two little girls as they made their early visit.

But spring came round, as always, even though the old queen was dead and her splendid funeral over. Long rows of produce, lettuce, radish, spring onion, cabbage, cauliflower, stretched across the level earth. George Parkinson called on his brother-in-law again to confirm arrangements for borrowing the horse and cart and set out with Prince, the dapple-grey pony, on his market rounds, going to Selby on Mondays, then fifteen miles to York on a Saturday, if the load warranted it. And Miriam kept him constant company. How she loved to 'help' her Dada. It was a wonder anything got done. Such a quiet child she was then, hardly speaking, taking everything in, so wordless that Mama began to worry and even went so far as to stop Doctor Summers in the street one day, so saving a seven shillings and sixpence consultation fee. 'Why won't Miriam talk? She's almost old enough for school. Is something the matter with her?' Doctor Summers gave a little, inward smile . . . 'She'll have enough to say, soon enough, Mrs Parkinson . . . You'll be wishing she'd be quiet. Now don't worry.' Mama went back inside the house.

Summer came, the goats were out in the far pasture and Miriam enjoyed the milking ritual. Every evening, when Dada had cleaned his tools and put them away, he would open the stable door. Kruger was always with him, but now Kruger sat at his feet, eyes fixed on his face, still and intent. Dada would take his watch out of his waistcoat pocket and look at it, turn to Kruger and say 'Nah then, lad.' Kruger was cocked, muscles tense. 'Go fetch them goats!' Kruger was off to the second meadow. He knew how to lean on the gate latch to open it. Then he barked, only once, and the goats came, Kruger following. There were six, grand, nanny goats. Five of them, Rose, Lily, Pansy, Daisy and Marguerite, were a normal brown, but Violet was different. Violet had a strong personality, was black all over, and, rarest of all, she had a single horn in the middle of her forehead. Miriam was very fond of Violet, despite her odd little ways, and satanic colour, and was convinced she must be related to the unicorn of her fairy tales.

Violet led the procession of goats into the stable. Dada stood beside an old table. There were two or three wooden steps on each side. Violet leapt lightly onto the table, stood calmly to be milked, then leapt down. The other goats followed. When the milking was over Kruger took the goats back and shut the gate after them. Then he came and stood in front of Dada, tongue hanging out, until Dada said, 'good lad.' Then he was happy. The milk went to Selby maternity hospital.

Summer days slid by in that regular pattern, so familiar to Miriam for it covered all her life, and with autumn came her start at school. Starting was as easy, natural and inevitable as everything round home and in Hemingbrough. The red school with its round-headed windows intersected by gothic arches, the high schoolroom inside, was a familiar place, not a hundred yards down Finkle Street from her home. She had swung on the gate and watched the other village children pass for years. They knew her and she knew them, and, though her conversation came in gusts of chatter broken by long silences, she was a quick-minded child who found her letters easy to pick up.

One autumn day, when Miriam was playing with her little sister May, after school was over, her Dada came over and said, 'Come on, my honeys, I'm going to show you two new babies.' 'I want to come,' said May. 'Aye, it's for both of you.' Dada picked them up, high in the air, one on each shoulder. It was like riding an elephant, but safe, not strange. To be on Dada's shoulder, his strong arm round her and holding tight against his neck, that was heaven. They rode over to the old cow-house, and Dada pulled the top half of the door open. The most beautiful babies were inside, so long-legged, soft and creamy-white in colour. Miriam was allowed to fondle them under the chin, and it was soft as duck's down. They were unsteady on their feet, and kept falling over, which made the girls giggle. Their little humps were smooth to the touch, and mother dromedary didn't seem to mind the girls talking to her new-born twins. It was lovely.

Mr Bostock, who ran the touring menagerie, heard the exciting chatter and came to speak to Dada. 'Looking at the new bairns, George?' 'Aye, they're a fine pair.' They spoke for a while about the other animals, Jingo the Burmese elephant, the ponies and zebras and the two barred wagons, cages on wheels, where hyenas and wolves paced restlessly and disturbed the children at night with their howling. An unearthly sound in rural Hemingbrough, one that made Miriam and May cower under the sheets in delicious, safe, terror, their minds running to jungles, and savage, foreign lands.

Mr Bostock stopped every year on the way to Hull Fair, to rest his animals. 'Now, about that goat,' said Mr Bostock to Dada, one George to another. 'I want her, you know. She'd look grand in procession and to show.' 'Well, I'm not thinking of parting with her,' said Dada. 'You'll get good money for her . . . and you know I'm fond of animals. She'll have a good home.' 'Well, I'll think on it,' said Dada. The conversation was over.

Next year Mr Bostock came again and made Dada a firm offer. 'Have you still got that goat?' 'Aye.' 'Well, I still want her . . . I'll give thee eight guineas.' Now Dada had already been thinking of the good working relations he had with George Bostock. It was on his conscience a little to see him right. And eight guineas was not a sum to turn down lightly. So at length they shook hands on the deal. Miriam watched Violet go, one of the long train of menagerie animals, led out before the ponies and zebras. How she cried. Losing Violet was like losing a sister. It was breaking up the home. All Dada could say was, 'Come on, honey, stop crying, do.' But she wouldn't stop. After all, Dada was being cruel and for some days she wouldn't go out to see the goats being milked, because Violet wasn't there.

It may have been Violet's departure for a public career, and the consequent need to look for a replacement, or the fact that he had money to hand, but one evening Dada sat longer than usual immersed in the unwieldly, buff pages of the *Yorkshire Evening Post*. He had been poring over the black type of private advertisements for a good hour, as the clock ticked and Kruger snored in front of the fire, until at last he sat up. 'That's it,' he said, and read out an advertisement to Mama. 'Marchioness of Tavistock's pedigree herd. Major, a three year old billy. Cream-coloured. In excellent condition.' They were going to have their own billy goat!

Major arrived by train, and Dada had to collect him from the station a couple of miles away. When the girls came back from school he was already shut in the stable. They sat down to lunch, for Mama expected them to be always on time. The children were not allowed to speak at mealtimes, but on this occasion the excitement was much too great. Miriam said, 'Dada, can we go and see the new billy?' Her Dada frowned and shook his finger at her. 'Get on with your dinner!' Then he relented a little, and explained. 'That goat has been travelling all morning and he's tired. He'll have to be left quiet.' Miriam wriggled in her chair and looked disappointed, but she didn't dare speak. 'You don't understand. He'll have to be left quiet in the old stable because he's been on the railway all morning.' Then Dada looked at them both in his kindly way, for if he was a fault-finder he was also a fault-mender, and he said, 'I promise, when you come home from school this afternoon, I'll take you both to see the new billy.'

But Miriam felt cheated. She just didn't want to wait. The school bell had started to ring, and they were going out of the back door and across the yard when she heard a bleating from the stable. How could she bear not to look. Guilty, but determined, she pushed the door a little and looked inside. There stood Major. He was lovely, cream-coloured, almost white underneath, and with a great, long, silky beard that reached almost to the ground. He was so fine that Miriam couldn't resist going to talk to him. She would just do as she did with the other goats, rub his head a little and give him a pat. But Major wanted to be left alone. He bleated fiercely, head down. Then he thrust with his horns, caught Miriam's dress, tossed once, and threw her high, almost to the ceiling. She came down screaming in surprise. Dada was into the stable like a shot. When he saw that she was unhurt, just shocked, he showed no sympathy to his disobedient daughter. 'Now what did I tell thee! Get up! Come on now, get off to school!'

Happenings of that sort, moments of such drama were memorable events in the prosperous, secure and happy round of Miriam's childhood. The regular, increasing work must be done, changing with the seasons, keeping the family busy inside the house as well as out of it. The brick floors had to be scoured and coloured up with blocks of rudd. On washing days they hauled buckets of water from the draw-well to the scullery to boil in a copper set-pan. Mama decorated the hearth-stone with blue pottery-mould. As winter closed around them the waiting for Christmas seemed interminable. The year died slowly, as old cabbage heads turned to slimy lumps on their stalks. With harder weather a wild cat took shelter in the granary, and the mice were less of a trouble. It was candles to bed and oil-lamps in the kitchen and parlour. The first flurries of snow sometimes brought Miriam memories of when she was a little girl and heard the bells tolling for Queen Victoria.

Then, at last, it was really Christmas, and she could lie in bed, watch the brass knobs vanish as the candle guttered, and feel May stirring beside her. More waiting, wanting, longer, so it seemed than any time before, until, with a rustling noise, the pair of her Dada's big stockings were suddenly filled. She dared not open her eyes, but lay in tense watchfulness for at least a minute, until at last she could lean forward, sleepily, just to make sure, feel the mysterious, crinkling shapes, then go to sleep right grand.

On Christmas Day Mama was busy getting the dinner ready. She always laid five places that day. As dinner-time drew near, Dada would stand at the door in his best suit, hands in his pockets. He believed strongly in his duty to the unfortunate, to the stranger within the gates, and when a tramp came by, his basin hanging on a stick over his shoulder, Dada would call to him, 'Come on, lad, there's some dinner here for thee.' When dinner was ready, Dada stood at the head of the table for grace. 'Christ is the head of this house, the unseen guest at every meal and the silent listener to every conversation.' Mind you, the children were not allowed much conversation, and the astonished tramp generally ate his food in silence. When dinner was over Mama would put together some of the remnants and send him on his way with his basin full.

Boxing Day always began early, for George Parkinson's great love, after his family, was music. He played cornet, euphonium and clarinet and had brought together a makeshift band in Hemingbrough. On Boxing Day they went the rounds of all the village houses and outlying farms to play carols. In reward they were given ducks, geese, stand-pies, rounds of cheese and the odd glass of rum. But the carol feast began, always, in Finkle Street, where May and Miriam would lean sleepily out of their window to watch the large figure of Dada, dim in the dawn-light, as he led his band with gusto into the high cornet notes of his favourite carol, 'Hail, smiling morn'.

Hail, Smiling Morn

Miriam sat at peace in the tall-spired church of Hemingbrough, her father's bunch of giant carrots lodged on a windowsill before her, for it was Harvest Festival. Idly she wondered if they might fall. She was thirteen years old and had stayed on after normal school-leaving age to help with the little children. She was a good scholar, quietly taking in a great deal, learning to speak more correctly, without the broad roughness of her uncles John or Thomas, though girls found proper language easier than boys. But it was a question now of what she should do next, a long drawn-out train of thought to while away the sermon. Most girls went into service, if they could get a place, others went to stay with relations in the industrial towns of West Yorkshire, where there was more work for women. Mother's sister lived in Bradford, and her daughter, Mabel, Miriam's cousin, she knew, was just of an age with her and already learning to be a dressmaker. But she couldn't leave her Dada, nor the house, and Kruger and the goats, and, of course, Mama. Miriam sat, dreaming through the service, to be stirred by May's plump elbow as the blessing was given. She rose automatically, blinked, and noticed an elderly couple, farmers apparently, from far out in the parish, looking inquisitively across the aisle at them. Then she heard the whispered comment; 'Them's George Parkinson's daughters.' 'Aye, bonny bairns aren't they.' She smoothed her dress down, pretending not to hear, but she knew they were right.

Life seemed to hang in suspense as that year ran its course. School and childhood were closing down, but she still blew the half-past eight dandelion before school, still stared through the arch-headed windows of the schoolroom at the sunshine outside. When Mr Rhodes, the flour-mill owner, came in his green-aged bowler and flour-spotted baggy trousers to scatter halfpence outside the school gate at four o'clock on a Friday, Miriam stood by and helped him restrain the greedy ones with his shepherd's-crooked walking stick, and she smiled at the babies' antics. Miriam was beginning not to think of herself as a bairn any more.

Of course there were more things she could do at home. When the cycling clubs came round that summer, and stopped for tea on Sundays, Miriam would look after them for Mama, settle them down on rustic seats beside the draw-well, close against the tall heads of the Turk's cap lilies, and bring them ewers of tea, home-made tea-cakes, and curd tarts. Then the gentlemen would unbutton their breeches at the knee, draw a little bottle of rum from their waistcoat pockets and lace the tea, whilst the ladies were penetrating the mysteries of the lilac and laburnum bower. May and Miriam gave each lady a little bouquet of flowers before they left, and they tied them to their handlebars.

One thing, only, seemed changed that thirteenth winter. Her Dada seemed tired, slower, almost old at times, which was hard to credit. No longer the wonderful figure of masculine strength, never tired, never irritable, never despondent, that she relied on as a child, a man who thrived on hard work, early rising, fresh air, plain food and righteous living. If he came home, wet, from market, he might sit before the fire and doze for an hour, rather than going right on with his work as he used to do. He might even have a sharp word for the loving daughter who wanted to chat with him. As winter drew to a close, Mama became more and more concerned about his condition. Their family talk about Dada's health drew out the fact that he had once been nearly at death's door. Could it happen again?

During the first Boer War, before Mama and Dada were married, a sad convoy had passed through the village. It contained sick and dying soldiers from the war, brought back by sea to Hull and travelling homeward, many of them infected with typhoid fever. Some arrived dead in Hemingbrough. They must be buried right away and the parson called for volunteers. With his strength, goodwill and unmarried state, who but George Parkinson should prove willing. He helped unload the corpses from the cart, carried them to the grave and stood respectfully through the service. The place of their common burial was carefully railed off. The convoy trailed onwards. George Parkinson fell ill presently, of a high fever with complications. His heart was affected. He was not expected to live, but his strength pulled him through.

Now his heart was troubling him again, and this old story came up. Mama was greatly worried. On Good Friday he had to stay in bed. On the Saturday he was weakening fast. The girls did not know what to do. They kept to the house, listening to every sound from the sick room. May was forever falling on her knees, saying, 'Please God, don't let Dada die.' It nearly drove Miriam mad, for she was too shaken to speak, and she was Dada's favourite.

Early in the evening Mama called her into the kitchen and gave her a little bottle. 'Go round to the Half Moon love, and ask Mrs Thomas for a drop of brandy.' Miriam stared. She was never allowed near the pub. Mama pushed her off rather tetchily. 'Go on, Miriam. If Mrs Thomas asks your age, say you'll be fourteen tomorrow.' Miriam, dazed, not really knowing what she was doing, walked right round the corner and into the public bar. The room fell silent, but she hardly noticed. Mrs Thomas took the bottle. She said nothing about Miriam's age, just filled it and asked, 'Is your Dada no better?' Miriam shook her head and her eyes filled with tears, until she could barely see the door. The sound of talking did not begin again until she was well outside.

Mother and daughters sat in the parlour that evening, not speaking, simply listening, hearing all the sounds of the house, waiting, perhaps, for a voice from upstairs. Every now and then Mama got up and went to the bedroom. Shortly after midnight, on Palm Sunday morning, the girls could hear Mama trying to talk to him, and his cracked voice singing out, feebly but clearly, 'Hail Smiling Morn, Hail.' He must be dreaming it was Boxing Day. Colder and later into the morning the girls huddled by the fire, and heard Mama coming downstairs. There was something different in her tread, a heavy, ominous note. Miriam couldn't speak, but she said to herself, 'I know what that means.' Mama came into the parlour. 'Your Dada's gone,' she said.

The rituals of burial were unchanged, except that someone other than George Parkinson had to toll the death bell. The vicar came and looked at him in the coffin on Monday morning. He said he wasn't satisfied and it would have to go back. Mr Snowden, the joiner, always kept three in stock, male, female and child, and Dada had always tolled the last few pulls as a message, first a short pause, then three for a child, six for a woman, nine for a man. Most folk in Hemingbrough knew who was at risk. When the coffin came back it had an inscription, 'The spirit shall return unto God who gave it'.

Uncle William, Uncle Thomas, Uncle George and Uncle John bore the coffin to the grave. Then it was back to the house for a funeral tea and such a sense of emptiness. There seemed no future to be had, as if the whole world they had built had died with Dada. Miriam wasn't sure she would ever be able to rely on a man again. The misery of being deserted was too great. A girl of fourteen is very vulnerable to such a grief, and she was to miss her Dada all her life.

Cousin Mabel from Bradford had sent them two black blouses, v-necked for Miriam, square cut for May, who was bigger built, and they wore them to the funeral. The house seemed unbelievably desolate as they worked at clearing-out and selling-off. Under the lease they had six

24

months to harvest the crops and remove their own fittings, but no other right to stay on. And how could Mama run the market garden on her own, with Miriam and May to help? It was out of the question. So the decision was taken, of itself, out of necessity. They would go to Bradford, stay with Uncle and Aunt, and find work for mother and Miriam where work was to be had. It was hard to believe they might never see Hemingbrough again, would certainly never live in the old home, and see the goats, hear the cockerels crowing, and Dada with his spade in the early morning. At least in a new place the memories wouldn't be too painful. Everything in Hemingbrough echoed thoughts of Dada.

The neighbours gathered to see them off in Uncle's trap. It was better to be away, to have an interest in the future again. They settled Mama comfortably, she was still crying, and looked round at their bags and boxes. Goodbyes and good wishes sent them away, to be followed by one more sobering comment from a particularly sanctimonious neighbour, 'I hope you'll always live a good life.' A good life, thought Miriam, and wondered if that might already be in the past. She shut her eyes and ran over the old house again, from Cockpit apple-tree to parlour cupboard. But then she kept seeing her Dada about the place, so she opened them. They had reached the railway station. The spire of Hemingbrough Church gradually sank into the horizon as the train took them on towards Bradford.

The Back-washing Machine

It was odd, very odd perhaps, but for two girls at fourteen and ten there was something exciting about this adventure to the big city, even though they left all their past behind them. The train journey had begun through countryside just like home; flat, arable land, red-brick villages, bridges crossing the sluggish Ouse. Not very different from the only other train journey Miriam had ever made, when the vicar of Hemingbrough organized a family outing to Bridlington.

Miriam could remember it as if it were yesterday. The one feeling seemed to melt into the other, as if it were the same train. The feeling of excited anticipation was the same. But then she had been only eight years old. It was really long ago. How she had stared out of the window, expecting to see the sea at every curve of the track, watching the telegraph wires go up and down. It was Dada's birthday the next day and Mama had said, 'We must get Dada to walk on,' when they got out at Bridlington and saw the shops. They went to the beach, and the lads from Hemingbrough rushed onto it, shouting, 'Ooh, what grand soil!' Mama managed to get Dada to walk with the vicar and they slipped into a shop. They bought him a most lovely purse with the Bridlington arms in blue and white enamel. They had dinner in a splendid kiosk right by the sea, with pillared and mirrored walls. There were four rooms full of folk from Hemingbrough and around. She had never wanted that day to end. But it had been her first holiday, the only trip away, and Dada had been there.

Now, as she looked out of the carriage window, the landscape was beginning to change. Hills appeared, and towns, houses with walls and roofs of stone, mills, chimneys, smoke, noise. It seemed to be a different world, and not like Yorkshire at all. Leeds swallowed the countryside, enormous and black, going on beside the track without relief, and Bradford merged into it like an added confusion. There was not the clarity of her own landscape, where villages and farms stood apart, circled by green; Selby, Howden, even great York itself, where Dada had gone to market.

At last, after miles of streets, and a cab to pay, they reached Auntie's house, with its oilcloth floors smelling of wax, the electric bulb hanging from every ceiling, and a proper bathroom with a fixed bath instead of the fire-side and a tin tub. It made Hemingbrough seem old-fashioned, slow and dull. Auntie gave Mama a kiss, and Mama sat down, closed her eyes as if she were never going to open them, and had a cup of tea.

Mabel showed the girls round. She was just a few months older, but she was so much more knowing, being at work already as a dressmaker in a big store right in the heart of the city. But Mabel was a goodhearted lass, sad for the fatherless girls, and full of fun. Miriam shared her bed, and they would giggle half the night on Sundays, playing with the little dog under the covers. Then Monday morning, oh, Monday morning, when Mabel had to be at work by seven and Auntie banged on the door at six. Then it was time to bury sleepy heads under the bedclothes and refuse to see the grey drizzle outside, the rising pall of smoke from mill chimneys. Until a voice scraped up the stairwell, 'Mabel! Mabel! Are you up! You'll miss breakfast, Mabel!' Almost giggling, even at that hour, Mabel would emerge from the clothes, yell 'Coming', and rap with her shoes on the floor beside the bed until it sounded as if she were up and about. What a change from Hemingbrough.

Bradford was full of wheels and clogs with a pawnshop in every road and trams in the streets and even motor cars. When she had to get up for work, later on, Mama bought an alarm clock at Morley's in Otley Road for one shilling and sixpence . . . no dandelion time. The food was so different, no big larder in the house, no granary, no pig in its sty or hanging as a side of bacon. Instead, hard and soft roes from the fishmongers eaten with piano-keys of fried bread, and the inevitable argument, 'Who's turn for the hard roe?' All the ready-cooked foods were always to hand, as in Mrs Robert's pie shop in Godwin Street with its vast, artificial pie illuminated in the window, always steaming and bubbling, advertising a plateful for twopence. Strangest of all, buying fruit and vegetables from a greengrocer for good money, rather than asking Dada to bring them when he came in from the garden. Discovering Bradford ways was very exciting, so were the shops, and the goods, the rows of fine silk dresses where Mabel worked, and the shawls, and shoes, and the clogs that ordinary working folk wore on their feet. Though when she came home from an expedition Miriam always found a rim of sooty grime around the collar and cuffs of her blouse.

But Mama was still very quiet. It wasn't so easy for her to settle down to the change, and she didn't really like not being in her own house. She had grown used to having her own things round her. Auntie had found her a temporary job as companion to an old lady, and so she left them for a while, to weep alone in the long nights and see her daughters on Sundays. The next question was, what to do with Miriam. No doubt about it, she had to work, and there was work to be had. But she was only a country lass, thin and quiet, not bred to mills, to mill-life, to the noise, crowds and mechanical, monstrous labour.

Miriam was first sent, on trial, which sounded rather like a criminal prosecution, to a pattern-card shop. The rows of girls sat at tables winding wool samples round stiff cards, their fingers moved at amazing speed and they seemed to be able to talk, look around, and laugh, without noticing what their hands were doing. So Miriam was sat down among them and told what to do. She was too shy to talk, though the girls weren't unfriendly, and her hands felt so clumsy, and she had such little fingers that she couldn't get an easy spin round the card. At the end of the week the manageress sent Miriam back to Mama with a note saying, 'This girl will not prove satisfactory.' Mama was upset, because she had now arranged to rent a small, terrace house, and money was going out all the time. They didn't have that much left from the sale of the market-garden stock and it was unthinkable to have nothing but their own poor earnings to live on. Their capital must be eked out as long as possible. Miriam was rather down-hearted after this first failure, but they had to try again.

So Auntie fixed up for her to have another trial, this time at a wool-spinning mill, where the money was better, but the work harder and the conditions more unpleasant. So Miriam found herself inside the grim walls of one of those prison-like mills that lined the streets of Bradford. This was even more of a trial, for there were girls younger than herself who looked as if they had been working there all their lives. They slid up and down the 'gait' between the machines, fitting empty bobbins, removing full ones, deftly re-winding the threads to take into the spinning processes. Belts thrashed, the spun fibres whirred in and out of the complex machinery and fattened onto the bobbins. Miriam was distracted by noise, heat and movement. She never seemed to be able to get to a bobbin in time. At the end of that long day the overlooker came up to her as she stood in the gait and the machines subsided into silent immobility on either side. 'Tha can't do this, tha knows,' he said, not unkindly. Miriam stood and looked at him. 'Nay, Nay,' he repeated. 'Th'art no good to us . . . get on with thee!'

Miriam couldn't go back to Mama again without a job. It would be too much to bear. Mama cried so easily now. So, made brave by desperation, she talked to a woman called Eliza Slater who lived nearby. She could confide in Eliza somehow, because she was one of those people who are always cheerful, friendly, welcoming others' troubles. Eliza was blind in the left eye, deaf in the right ear and had a bad leg, so that she limped about like a duck with a broken wing. A game duck, all the same, and always quacking bravely. Eliza had worked thirty-seven years in the wool-combing shed, where greasy raw wool was prepared for spinning.

'Now, tha must come along wi' me, love,' she told Miriam. 'Tha'll get more brass . . . and Harry'll move thee on when tha suits.' So she took Miriam back, right away, to speak to Harry Baker in the old, dirty shed, with its broken floor and the matting of dusty fibres everywhere.

Harry told her to come back next day, and when she did it was even more alarming than the spinning shed. Hot, sweaty, with the steam from washing the wool and with so much stuff in the air you had to keep a hand over your mug of tea to stop it filling with hair. The noise, too, was dreadful, and you could only hear if people shouted.

Miriam shrank into herself and looked at Eliza for encouragement. Harry said, 'Is there owt you can do?' Miriam began to shake her head. She hadn't much faith in her own capacity by now. Then she thought of Mama, and the tears. 'I can try, can't I, please,' she said. She said it so quietly that Harry must have read her lips. Anyway, he nodded, took her arm to lead her to another part of the shed, and shouted, 'I've a lass here as'll show thee how to go on.'

So she began alongside Eliza, 'can-dodging', as the lengths of combed wool were run out into large metal cans ready for the spinners. The weight must be exact, the heavy cans were always waiting to be changed, take off the full, put on the empty ones. It was stiflingly hot at times, up to a hundred and twenty degrees, though welcome in winter when they hadn't coal to spare for a fire. The 'fly' hovered everywhere, like a cloud of long-legged insects, lit up where shafts of sunlight penetrated the whitewashed panes in the saw-edged roof. At times it got into the mouth and lungs, so that Miriam would cough up the bits for half an hour or so when she got home. But at least this was a job she could do, not too clever for her, and it brought home good money to Mama who really needed it.

Harry was a good foreman, not just an overlooker, but a man who saw you right if you were a willing worker and would stand by you if you got into trouble through no fault of your own. One day Annie Walsh didn't turn up. Harry stopped Miriam as she was starting up on the can-winder. 'Come along, Miriam, tha must learn t' backwash.' 'Oh, Harry,' said Miriam, for at fifteen she shrank from any new challenge. Change had become a threat. But Harry gentled her along to the backwashing room, filled entirely by the processing machine. Out of the big cans came the combed wool in thick, greyish strands, through rumbling iron rollers, down into a square vat bubbling with soapy water, out again, round a roller, down again into another vat that seethed with Reckitt's blue, then, dripping blue as it ran, round drying rollers in a figure of eight pattern until at last it vanished again into another great can, to be taken along to the can-winder. Miriam looked at this monster machine, the constant motion, the steam filling the room, hissing and bubbling of the vats, thudding grind of the rollers. She felt her hands clenched tight in her apron pockets.

'Tha must keep on walking around, Miriam,' said Harry. 'Don't just stop at this end . . . tha must go and see if it's all right that end.' He took her to the drying cylinders and showed her the window of thick glass that allowed her to keep an eye on that part of the process. All that morning Harry was there to help her learn.

But next day she was on her own. After the first feelings of terror Miriam actually began to manage this new job and to feel a little confidence in working on her own. In fact she even began to hum a little hymn to herself as she stacked the full cans by the far end of the machine. Then something made her turn. She heard a shout above the noise of the machine. Another lass was waving her arms at her excitedly, and she hurried over. 'Miriam, there's a mullock this end!' She looked in horror. Wool was winding round the rollers, caught up somehow, getting into a thicker tangle by the minute and the rollers were being forced apart as it grew and bulged at an alarming rate. She stared in panic. It seemed as if the machine had come alive, was about to expand and devour everything in the room. Miriam was shaking all over. She stood, stared, then remembered what she must do, and rushed to the handle beside the drive-pulley. One heave and the belt slackened, power was cut off, and everything ground to a groaning halt. She looked around fearfully. It would be dreadful telling Harry, and making the inevitable visit to Mr Hird, the manager, with his fierce eyes. Mr Hird would take no excuses. She would probably get the sack, and a bad name in the trade to go with it.

Harry came. He stood and looked at the tangle of wool round the unseated rollers. He looked back at Miriam and shook his head. Then he took out a thick-bladed pocket knife and attacked the mess. The soft wadding came away in great lumps, and soon the rollers were clear, could be re-seated and the broken ends threaded through the machine. Miriam stood and waited. Harry grinned, shook his head again, said, 'Don't forget, Miriam, keep looking yon end,' and went back to the main shed. Miriam watched the back-washing machine extremely carefully. It was only at night, in bed, that she woke up and began to cry with relief.

This interminable life of work and home and a little play went on year after year. Miriam grew older. There was not much to exercise the imagination in the wool-combing shed, and somehow she wasn't much interested in men. The lads she met didn't have much to them. Mama looked after the house, grew older, year by year and died. May got married and left. Miriam was alone, with the memories of Hemingbrough to fill her mind. Often, quite clearly, she could see her Dada as he organized the races at the village sports, strong, respected and very fair. See him in the sunlight of the open fields with the church spire in the distance. Then his voice and words would ring in her head. 'The same bairns shouldn't have to be winners all the time.' She found herself blinking back the tears.

Jack Carl

and Sheffield

The heart of steel, as it was in Edwardian days, Sheffield has always been very much its own, peculiar place. The city crowds into a jumble of steep valleys at the eastern edge of the Peak District in the very South of Yorkshire. Overtopped by the hills, it looks out across the lowlands, and its heavy supplies have traditionally come in by canal barge from the Humber ports.

Sheffield folk are well known to be as idiosyncratic as their city. Above all, the skilled men of the cutlery trade, the independent 'little mesters' who made the Sheffield knives, famous since Chaucer's time. They were 'the craftiest devils I've ever known in my life,' according to Jack Carl. He should know, for he was one of the best of them. Jack was born in Sheffield in 1906, has always lived and worked in the city, wheel to wheel with his fellow grinders. He is grinding to this day.

Sparks

The bar steel glowed orange-red as his Dad struck a series of deliberate blows with the nine-pound hammer. It was like watching a tree grow, the flakes of greying metal forming temporarily on the face as he struck, then fading back into the blazing matrix. Dad had forged it down to a taper, now he was pulling out the edge with carefully directed blows. 'Th'art taking t'guts out of it,' said Jack. He never minded who he spoke to or what he said. His Dad grunted. The scale was cracking off now as the blade cooled, but he was nearly there. 'What's it going to be?' 'Salmon knife,' said Dad, 'Hudson's Bay Company.' It certainly was a hefty blade, still a quarter inch thick at the back edge, over a foot long and forged to an elegant curve. 'It'll take off a salmon's head wi' one blow . . . a grand blade this.'

Dad swung it through the air, just by way of demonstration, and laid the tang on his stiddy. The beaked anvil with its cast-in slots and bosses and its gait-holes for working complex shapes, was so patterned that it looked like a cubist painting. 'It takes a nebbed tang,' said Dad, as he cut off the surplus bar with a couple of blows of hammer on cold chisel. 'Just lean on t'bellows.' Jack hurried to help. He liked watching the small-grained coke suddenly glow-up with heat in the raised hearth as he worked the bellows lever. It was pleasant to feel the heat on his face like this on a cold morning, half an hour before school. Dad re-heated the tang to a dull red, then hammered it into a curved beak at the end. Jack looked, inquisitively. 'Aye, 'tis a big neb, lad. I'm told they need a fair weight under the hand to stun them salmon before they chop 'em.' He demonstrated a quick blow with the heel of the hand, then a slice with the blade. 'Cutler'll fix it wi' brass neb-ends . . . gives more weight.' Dad laid it aside.

'Well, that's one done. I've two gross to forge altogether. Lean on t'bellows again, lad. When school's over tha can take what's done down to t'grinders . . . Jack Rains in Radford Street'll do it.' Jack grinned at his Dad. The grinders were his friends, a lot more fun than school. He could stand and watch the sparks fly from their wheels for hours, well, minutes anyway, until they let him have a go. Jack was strong for his age and didn't reckon much to lessons. He preferred the great showers of sparks cascading from four-foot sandstone grinding-wheels as the forged blade was forced against it.

'Art' still here?' 'Aye, Dad.' 'What for? Day-dreaming? . . . Get off to school – and be quick at dinner time . . . go on . . . shog off.' Jack took a last look round the grimy shop, a lean-to shed among the houses at the back-end of Beet Street, where Dad worked as a little mester. He had four men working as hand forgers to sog into the hot metal alongside him. Jack worshipped his Dad. He could handle a nine-pound hammer all day, till eight at night if need be, and yet could be gentle as a kitten, with his pigeons especially. One last look at the fire, the grimy hearth, heaps of rammel in the ash-holes, and the soot-stained walls. It was warm inside. 'Get off to school.' His Dad raised the hammer, and Jack was off.

School wasn't worth mentioning, but Jack was back at dinner time. Dad was clearing a bit of space to lay out the salmon knives, not cleaning up, for that was rarely done. They had once had a factory inspector in, asking when the shop was last whitewashed. Dad looked at him, 'Not in my time.' 'You're William Hunter?' 'That's right, Billy Hunter they call me.' 'Well, Mr Hunter, it's the law.' 'Aye, ask young Will, over there, when it were done last . . . he's been about, on and off, for sixty year or so.' But young Will didn't know when they last put 'bug-blindin' on the walls. He certainly hadn't seen it. The inspector went away in despair. It was the same all over Sheffield. Up every back street was a row of little workshops where one stage or another of the cutler's craft was carried out, from forging to grinding, buffing, polishing and hefting. They were free men, little-mesters all, and, like Jack's Dad, they didn't take kindly to interference.

Jack and his Dad walked home. They lived in a better area of Sheffield, up to the north of the crowded valley behind the Town Hall where the workshops were. In Crookes there was more air, and Beedley Street was at the top, close to Bole Hill, the recreation ground and old quarries, and overlooked by the steep-sided heights of the Peak District. It was a good place for pigeons, that was why Dad had bought the house, and he had a forty-foot long pigeon cote, beautifully built in slatted wood, at the bottom of the garden.

'Dad,' said Jack. He had something to clear up, now that they were both men together, something he hadn't felt like mentioning first thing in the morning when Dad had a big order on. But now pigeons were in the air. 'Dad.' 'Aye?' 'They want to put me in t'choir.' 'They what . . . who do?' 'My Mother, and Auntie.' Dad nodded. 'Aye . . . well that'll be because thy Aunt's in t' Salvation Army . . . and Alice is that way inclined as well. But what's wrong wi t'choir . . . Tha likes to sing.' 'Aye Dad, but it's three nights a week . . . they're driving me to religion!' Dad laughed. 'And . . . I'll not have time to look after t'pigeons.' Dad frowned. 'Tha'll stop wi' me,' he said, and, as soon as they reached home, he sent Jack down to the pigeon-cote and went directly inside.

Dad was laughing to himself when he came back. 'Well – there's an end of religion for thee, lad. But I don't know whether thy mam'll speak to thee, or give thee dinner for a week or two, though. What did'st say to t'vicar?' Jack grinned. 'I told him me mother'd popped me best clothes in t'pawnshop an I couldn't go to t'choir.' 'Did you now! No wonder she's right taken with thee . . . Vicar's been round asking her not to go poppin' clothes . . . She didn't know what he was on about!' Dad chuckled again. 'But I told her I needed thee to look after t'pigeons.'

Jack looked at his Dad. Dad winked. Somehow he could always get away with it, provided he did the pigeons right. 'Dad, that one's ailing.' 'Let's see.' Dad was serious at once. 'Aye, it's losing feathers . . . I've been wondering about him for a bit . . . Well, he's done well before, but there's no favourites in our cote.' Dad took hold of the half-protesting pigeon firmly, but gently. One quick twist of those muscular hands and it was over. 'Put him in t'bin.' They went in to dinner and Mother wouldn't speak to Jack.

'She'll come round,' said Dad on their joint way down to work and school. Jack wasn't much worried. He never did take much heed of what folk thought of him. 'Bear in mind, lad,' Dad added, 'she took thee in when thy father died. Hast' seen thy real mother, now and then.' It was a statement of fact, not a question. 'Aye.' 'Well, think on't. Alice, now, she's got more need to do right by thee than if she was a real mother. She can't take it for granted. Now, I'll not have thee driven to religion . . . but, think on it, now and then.'

After school Jack took the forged blades along to the grinders in Radford Street. Their workshops were even muckier than Dad's forge. The yellow swarf, compound of powdered stone and metal, thrown in a wet spray from the grindstones, covered walls and floor. It covered the grinders too, which was why they got called 'yeller-bellies', as each of them sat on his padded horsin-board, leaning forward to press the blade against the wheel and grind it to perfect, satin-smooth, sharpness. The shops were cold, with open half-doors to let in air. Many grinders died of 'grinders' asthma', an illness that rotted the lungs. Some thought it was caused by dust from the sandstone. There was always a lot of that dust to form the swarf; for a hard-working grinder could wear a four-foot wheel from the local quarries down into a two-foot, pocket-knife wheel in a couple of weeks. And it was always damp because of the water in the trow, the wooden trough that the wheel sat in. The wheel needed cooling and damping. A hot wheel would mark the steel so badly that you couldn't grind it out. The grinders coughed as they sat at their wheels, and they left the doors open because fresh air was known to be the best protection against TB.

'It's young Jack.' They always made him welcome. 'What's t'got this time, Jack?' 'Salmon knives.' 'My, they're a grand lot.' Jack stood, watching the sparks. 'Dos't fancy a go.' 'Aye.' 'Climb aboard, then.' Jack took his seat on the horsin and held the blade, exactly as instructed, against the revolving wheel. The sparks flew a couple of inches from his nose as the dull, forged steel, with its hammermarks, was transformed into a shining, polished and threatening weapon, as beautiful as a crusader's sword. 'We'll give thee a job, Jack . . . come and work wi' us! Here's sixpence for thee.' Jack got on well with the grinders. They had a happy-go-lucky way of life, a freedom, that he relished, light as the sparks from their wheels.

As he grew older Jack spent more time on errands for the grinders and for his Dad. The cutlery firms, who actually dealt in finished knives, got in orders and handed out work at the 'pickin-hole', were larger; they employed folk in some quantity, and were more awkward to deal with. When Dad had finished an order he would send Jack along on a Saturday morning to collect the money. They always kept him waiting. But one firm was particularly bad, and one Saturday he still wasn't paid by one o'clock. That was enough for Jack. He resented petty tyrannies and would do anything to make a mock of them. So he wrote 'Bet Shop' on the wall and went away.

'Hast got paid?' said his Dad. 'No,' said Jack, and told his tale. Dad went off to the cutlers. 'Where's my brass?' 'Never mind thy brass – hast seen what thy lad's wrote on t'wall?' 'Aye . . . he wants to go playing football . . . There's no cause to go keeping him here. Tha's got thy work . . . on time. Pay up on time! Never mind waiting till one o'clock!' The little mesters knew they were free men.

Jack reached ten years old and reckoned it was time he was free from school. He had no fear of work. Wasn't he Billy Hunter's adopted son? Didn't he know his way around all that labyrinth of grimy working streets in the bottom of Sheffield? All his life he had been picking up the feel of that complex society of craftsmen, the reliance of one trade on another, and the combination of their skills to produce a finished work of art. To Jack, work was freedom.

'I want to be a grinder, Mam.' She looked, hopelessly, at his Dad. 'Don't let him go to be a grinder, Billy. You know what they're like. Always drinking. Always mucky . . . and that coughing. You just have to hear 'em. If they go into Winter Street hospital, they're dead.' She had raised Jack since he was three weeks old, fed him well, bought his sailor suits, prayed over him. Now he was becoming a man, like Billy, and not listening to her. She looked at Billy. He didn't look back directly, but she had got her answer. 'If the lad wants to be a grinder . . .' That was all he said, but Alice knew it was no use arguing.

Jack found the sparks still drew him to the wheel. The lads at Radford Street offered to take him on when he talked over his plans with them during his last school holiday. It was a Monday, so no-one was actually contemplating work. 'Come on, Jack,' they said, 'let's go round to th' Eagle. We'll drink to thee and thy wheel.' Jack went along, happily, with his new mates, down into the cellar. 'Come on, Fanny, let's have a jug,' and Fanny brought up a white, enamel pitcher, two quart sized. They passed it round, each drinking in turn, Jack taking his part like a man and wiping the froth from his non-existent moustache with the best of them. That was another thing, his Mother didn't like the grinders' mucky beards and moustaches, the swarf mixing with the grease.

Jug followed jug, and Jack wasn't going to deny his manhood by falling out. He drank along with the rest, a veteran of ten years. The beer went down very well, though it made him talk too much and his belly felt a bit queasy after he'd had about two pints. 'Tha'll soon get used to it, lad,' they said, which was true enough. As he went home at tea-time the sparks were flying round inside his head. Mother took one look at him, grabbed him and shoved him off to bed. Working man or not he had to go. When Dad came home he could hear her sobbing and arguing with him downstairs. She had always known the grinders were a bad lot. Jack could feel his stomach heaving by now, but he wouldn't give in. At length Dad came upstairs and opened the door. They looked at each other. Jack wasn't feeling that good and Dad must have seen it, because there was a twinkle in his eye. All Jack said was, 'What else could I do?' before he closed his eyes and groaned. And Dad nodded. 'That's all right,' he said, in understanding, man to man, and went away again.

Water-canker

Dad had a word with Jack Rains. They found a trow to rent in Radford Street alongside the other grinders and young Jack was glad. 'Right,' said Dad to them all, 'he wants learning. But he'll never tell a tale . . . and if he does owt wrong – clip him!' Ten-year-old Jack was where he wanted to be, a free man, at work, and up to his elbows in sludge. He didn't have a great deal to learn. He was crippled with backache for a day or two from the hours of leaning forward against the wheel, but he got used to that, and it only returned now and then. He got 'hooves' on his hands, a sure sign of his working status, and, like every grinder, he had his yellow belly, sprayed with swarf. His mother used to groan at the sight. She still didn't approve of the work he was doing, nor of the ungodly company.

Jack was a natural grinder. From pocket-knife blades he soon graduated to bigger things, butchers' knives, farriers' knives and carvers. Fighting, at first, with a change of pulley when the belt failed to turn his wheel at a proper speed, he had to ask for help. But he soon learnt how to fit a new wheel, tall as himself, of solid sandstone nine inches wide, to bed it in well and lubricate the axle with mutton suet – nothing else held in place so well yet gave out grease when the axle heated up. You had to have a wheel running smooth and true, or there was no hope of grinding anything except a cuckoo. 'Eh – he's got t'cuckoo,' was what the lads said when he had work to do again. He made some mistakes, grinding carbon-steel too hot, so that he marked it with a white line. Then it was, 'This won't do, Jack,' and they docked him for it, and the cries of 'Cuckoo' sang through the shop. A new wheel cost eight pounds, and he was docked to pay for that, as well as trow rent, room and power. But there was no question of paying for heat. They didn't have any.

So Jack worked through into his teens, his hands numb in winter, sweating in the close, back-street workshop in summer. The grinders must work to live, but they had their own choice about how they did it. Calling each other every name under the sun, the grinders would go out drinking every Monday, without fail. The end of 'Saint Monday' saw the ceremony of 'fetching a grinder', which generally required a hand-cart and four of his mates, who stopped at every pub on the way home, but left the offender tied to the cart, just to think things over. Tuesday saw a slow start to the working week, not surprisingly, but after that it was a question of soggin it for all hours, using candles and oil-lamps, gaslight if they had it, the wheels spinning and backs bent to them.

Freedom and risk went together. Jack Rains was given a bad lot of blades to grind one day, poor metal at a poor price. 'These are cheap,' he muttered, scowling as he fought them against the wheel. 'They speak cheapness, nowt but sow metal.' He threw one down in disgust. 'And look what they're paying me. I'll just do one side on 'em. After all, I'm working a dead horse, anyroad.' He grinned in delight at the thought, for payment in advance meant they couldn't take the money back. He ground them one-sided and handed them in. All the shop were waiting when he came back. 'Well, what did they say to thee?' 'What dost' think? "Them won't do".' He mimicked the ware-housing girl's surprise. 'So I told 'em – I'll do no more at t'price . . . and left 'em . . . its sours anyroad.' Young Jack and the rest nodded approval, even though it meant they would get no more work from that firm – for a while at least. They were the craftiest devils, these grinders, as Jack was learning.

Frank Stenton got done the other way round, and that was more usual. He was just married. It was the week before Christmas, and he handed in a big order that would keep them going over the holiday. It was sweets, not sours, so he was to be paid on delivery. 'This won't do,' said the warehousing girl. There was one of the blades that they wouldn't take, just one. That meant he wouldn't get paid, for it was too late to re-grind it. No money for Christmas and Frank was reduced to borrowing from his father-in-law.

That was how they lived, and safety, health, the income from steady work, were all a grinder's own business. Jack learnt to buy his own wheels, check them over, settle them in, and run them at his own speed. He was no fool, even if he enjoyed his drink and the fun and games as a lad. But it happened, even so. A new wheel was spinning fast. The explosion, as it came apart at speed, caught him a tremendous blow in the belly and chest. Jack was thrown backwards over the trow, the horsin-board with him. He came to in a heap of sandstone fragments, his mates around him, and blood everywhere. His first thought was, 'That's eight pound gone!' Then he felt the pain. His right buttock and leg were carved open to the bone, his trousers ruined. They took him to the hospital. It couldn't be properly stitched and it was three months before he could sit on a horsin-board again. It was a good job he lived at home still. There was no workman's compensation for the self-employed.

It was even longer before he could sit on a bike saddle properly, which was a serious matter now that bikes had taken over from pigeons as Jack's hobby. He had high hopes of becoming a cycle racer, and the accident was bound to hold him back. But Jack was tough and he recovered fast. Earning well as a grinder, up to seven pounds a week after the first war was over, Jack bought himself a couple of racing bikes, then an open camshaft motorbike that would do fifty miles an hour in second gear.

He met a car manufacturer called William Morris on the racing circuit and they raced their bikes together. When he was twenty-six, Jack won a twelve-hour race across the flat countryside of Lincolnshire, covering a distance of two hundred and forty-eight miles in the time. After that triumph, his Dad bought him a new suit for the prize-giving, a fifty-shilling suit that fitted him a treat. His life suited him, at the wheel, in the saddle, or in the pub, and Jack thrived.

He was due to ride in a big race one Saturday afternoon, near Bawtry, so he went into strict training, biked to and from work every day and cut himself down to a pint for lunch. Early in the week he had got a spike of metal in his thumb, just a sliver from a blade he was grinding. It hardly bled, so he pulled it out with his teeth and carried on grinding in the week-old swarf. By Wednesday he had a sore, a swollen pap of yellowish flesh, that stung every time he used his thumb. By Friday half his thumb seemed to be rotten, his whole body throbbed with the pain. He couldn't sleep, but sat up in his bedroom, fiercely determined to race. The pain was enough to drive him mad; he couldn't bear to sit still and it throbbed worse when he moved.

Mother got up to go to the lavatory, he could hear the stairs creak. She must have seen his light on, because she looked in at the door on the way back. 'What's up, Jack?' He held out his thumb. 'Oh my goodness, just look at that! It has got worse, hasn't it? Why dids't'a not say owt? It's t'hospital for thee tomorrow my lad!' 'I'm going to that race, I can't go to t'hospital.' 'Thar't not!' 'I've trained for it . . . and . . .' Jack mistakenly waved his hand in argument. The pain nearly laid him out. Mother nodded. 'Come along, Jack . . . Be a good lad. It can't go on like this . . . Tha'll lose thy thumb.' Even though he was pigheaded, wouldn't put up with women's fussing and must be his own boss, Jack found this was an occasion when it was good to give in. 'Well, all right, Mam,' he said, 'I'll come to t'hospital with thee.' And when the door closed behind her, he added, 'and I'll go racing after!' But he still couldn't sleep for the pain.

She got him to surgery. The pain was dictating every decision by now. 'Well,' said the surgeon, 'that's as fine a water-canker as I've seen.' 'What are you going to do?' 'It must come out. Right away, to prevent it spreading. We shall have you under anaesthetic in a jiffy.' 'No, I'm going to a bike race.' The surgeon looked amusedly angry. 'It needs an immediate operation.' 'Well, cut it then! Cut it now . . . in cold blood . . . never mind nowt else.' Jack knew he'd never be able to race if he was groggy from the anaesthetic. The surgeon looked from Jack to mother, then back at Jack's determined face. Mother shook her head, wearily, but said nothing, knowing better than to argue with a working grinder. 'Very well, but it will certainly hurt,' said the surgeon with a shrug. As he laid out the scalpel, Jack noticed it wasn't well ground. He reckoned he could do better. Then he closed his eyes.

Hurt it certainly did. Half the ball of Jack's thumb had to go, and there was definitely a moment when he wondered if he had made the right choice. The room seemed to thunder past him just as if he was struck by a flying wheel and the slice of the scalpel through rotten flesh shrieked in his mind. Jack said nothing, though his breath hissed through clenched teeth. They bandaged him up at last. Then the surgeon said, 'I know you're a grinder, young man. I think you should clean up your equipment to avoid reinfection.' Jack couldn't help laughing, weak as he was. It wasn't done! No grinder ever emptied the water sludge from the bottom of his trow except when he was fitting a new wheel. Fey his trow just for a water-canker! What would his mates say? Jack grinned weakly in amusement at the surgeon's ignorance. The surgeon sighed and shook his head at mother once again. When they got home, Jack wheeled his bike round to the front. 'I'd best be off for t'train,' he said. 'You're mad,' said his mother. Whether she still thought it was worth praying for him, Jack didn't know, or care, but he won the race, though he was groggy afterwards.

The first prize was a mantel-clock with Westminster chimes, inscribed with the maker's name, Gill and Son of Sheffield. By then he had a collection of trophies and had begun to go regularly to Bawtry for the cycle races. Sometimes he stopped at Mrs Thomson's guest-house overnight, and there he met a farmer's daughter who came to help out with the teas. After a while Jack began to bike out there, thirty miles and back, on Friday evenings after work, just to see the lass and to get a little extra training in as well. It didn't pay to be soft, and on the whole he concealed any romantic notions behind a wisecracking exterior, but even a self-employed grinder can be vulnerable to life's amiable weaknesses at times. His mates at the grinding shop reckoned they knew what he was about and the atmosphere on Fridays was frowsy with suggestions about what kept Jack out so late – and why he was too weak to take his ale on Mondays.

They married, despite the wisecracks, and bought a house in Robertshaw Street, a stone-built, terrace house with two bedrooms and a back yard. Jack transformed it into a palace with an inside lavatory. They had a daughter, and he built a small pigeon cote in the yard, though the proper transmission of his family tradition meant that he must wait for a grandson. The Westminster-chime clock sat on the mantel in the front room and regularly gouged him out to work. Jack continued to earn a good living and they managed well throughout the depression of the thirties, when other folk, little mesters even, were on the scrap-heap. Then came the second war, and Jack was found to have a skill too valuable to be risked in combat. Instead he was directed to work for a firm of surgical instrument makers, grinding scalpels to meet an ever-increasing demand. He had his work cut out, for the surgeons were very busy. One day George Gills called him into the office. 'Can you start early, Jack, say seven o'clock for the next week or two? We're getting behind.' That meant getting up at six, which was not easy for a man who had been a free grinder and used to fixing his own hours. 'I'll try,' he said. 'Well,' answered Mr Gills, 'we'll need you. Dick lives nearby . . . I'll tell him to call for you in the morning.' 'All right, send him on,' said Jack. So Dick called, puffing a bit from the steepness of the hill, and they had a cup of tea whilst the Westminster clock chimed the half hour. Dick went over and looked it in the face. 'Time to get bloody workin',' he said, and they left the house.

Later in the morning George Gills called for Jack again. 'I thought we had a lot to do,' said Jack in his usual free and easy way. 'What's all this stopping and starting for?' Mr Gills looked at him with mild reproach. He seemed slightly embarrassed. 'Now then, Jack, I didn't think you'd rob me.' Jack was amused, then angry. 'I've never robbed anyone in my life!' 'I know you've got a West-minster-chime clock with Gill and Son on it . . . It must have come from here.' 'I didn't even know you lot made clocks as well!' In this unhappy situation Mr Gills preferred a moral reply to arguing over facts. 'It isn't right, Jack . . . just taking one . . . is it?' 'I haven't taken one! Damn it . . . what did I tell thee! It were a prize from t'National Cycling Union. I'll show thee!' Jack marched out of the office and the works. He wouldn't go back until his innocence was proved. And, in any case, with the workload they had on Gills desperately needed a grinder who could handle scalpels.

He found the old secretary of the local branch of the Cyclists Union. 'Dost remember that clock I won?' 'Aye – the Westminster chime?' 'That's right. I've been accused of thieving it.' 'Well, I'm buggered . . . Have you, indeed?' He was a slowish sort of fellow, a bit heavy, but after about half a minute's thought, he added, 'I'd best go along with thee.' They marched into the office like a military deputa-tion, ready to fight, but Mr Gills was duly impressed and apologized very decently for the mistake he had made. Jack found this galling because he reckoned he deserved a fight to relieve his feelings. In the end, he was fairly polite to Mr Gills, 'the daft bugger', but as for that creeping devil Dick, 'Don't send that fellow round to my house again . . . or he'll not shog back to thee!'

That was how Jack liked to talk to his boss, free and

easy, man to man, but with the advantage of stronger language. He didn't need any Union except the Cyclists. But the war, and then the peacetime revolution in life and industry, brought an end to Jack's traditional way of life. Cutlery gradually became a factory-made product. Trade unions moved into the disorganized and declining labour system. Council planners cleared the slum areas that housed both families and workshops. Jack's house, his palace, was bought out by 'the forty thieves' as he calls them, for twenty-eight pounds. His workshop went soon after. There were no shops to be had at a little-mester's rent and he would have to become a slave again, to work for an employer.

Fortunately, at Joseph Elliots, an old established firm, still making traditional cutlery, he found a refuge for his trow and traditions. At seventy-four years old, Jack leaves the pub late on Monday lunchtimes and returns to his wheel in the Victorian, brick workshop in Sylvester Street. His long-time friend, Harry, has a hand forge in the yard, which is just as his Dad's was, and Harry can wield a nine-pound hammer with the best of them. They make butchers' knives, carving knives, bone and horn handled, pocket-knives of all types and sizes, from lambsfoots to cold-finger knives. Jack can still fit a wheel with a bull's neck buffing leather, though he grinds on a composition wheel that won't fly apart like the old sandstone. He has his skills. His wife is dead, but he has his mates.

When Jack takes a dozen finished blades along, the warehousing lass may well say 'I don't think this'll do, Jack.' As a well-established craftsman, Jack will look at this slip of a girl, no more than forty in her headscarf, and wink lecherously. 'Bloody marvellous . . . there's a blade as'll cut for ever and ever amen, and she says it won't do.' He picks it up and looks along the edge till his eyes water. Then he sighs, for after all he did grind it after Harry had treated him at the pub. He'll just have to grind it over again. That's freedom for you.

Kit Calvert

and the Dales

The Dales are, for many people, the heart of traditional Yorkshire. Those green valleys are set in the moors, each with its sprinkling of grey stone villages and pleasant market towns. They represent the old, farming ways, the slow-moving patterns of rural life, centring round sheep pastures on the fells and dairy-farming in the valleys. It was never a rich life, the soil being too poor and the weather too harsh for grain to grow and ripen. Steep slopes, long distances on foot, simple food, were the lot of farmers and farmworkers in the Dales.

Kit Calvert grew up in Wensleydale, in the village of Burtersett, living a frugal life. He learnt his letters at Grandad Fothergill's knee, broke in his clogs by kicking stones, and could skin a sheep's head better than any lad in the village. Kit started work as a farmer's lad, learning all the old skills, from the use of a hay sledge to rowelling sick cattle. Wensleydale has always been the setting for his labours.

Quarryman's son

Just after first light in early winter-time, the screeching would grow louder and louder until Kit had to wake up. The quarry started at six, and as soon as the shire horses from the stables above Lowgate farm had been harnessed to the cart they set off down the road to Hawes station. The worked sandstone made a heavy load, seven tons stacked on edge the length of flat-bedded carts strengthened with two-inch boarding. The carts had small wheels, turning below the body of the cart, and as they ran down the steep streets of Burtersett a steel slipper was screwed under one wheel to act as a brake. How it squeaked down Middlegate, cutting a groove in the white water-bound road surface of crushed limestone, creating a channel for others to follow, and for lads like Kit to splash their clogs through when it rained.

That insistent screech had echoed through Kit Calvert's bedroom every working morning of his life. He needed no alarm clock; ten past six and that was that. Bob might lie on under the covers, but Bob was only just out of skirts, a younger brother and sleepier than Kit anyway. More and more now Kit was up early, not a baby any longer, but a serious working lad, the live-wire of the family, helping his father, about ready for school. Father worked in the quarry, along with most men in Burtersett. There must be a good eighty quarrymen, from skilled masons knapping the stone to lads barrowing the chippings to the tip. Maybe Kit would work there when he reached twelve years old. He knew the other lads who did. He might learn to work with the stone like his father. There was a good prospect in Yorkshire stone, it would always be needed.

When Kit went up the cart track from the village, up into the edge of the fells, where the vein of workable stone could be found, he came into a strange world of men and wilderness. The wide hills sloped up and away, over from Wensleydale into Ribblesdale, so much space for sheep and curlews. But in a small area of hillside the works of men fell on the senses, rap of stone-hammer, or ring of pick, shouts, whinnying of horses, smell of singeing, sight of spoil heaps. Carrying the tin bottle with his father's tea, Kit ran past them all, setting it to warm beside the blacksmith's fire, where picks were sharpened daily. The quarrymen laughed at his eagerness, but kindly enough, for he was in the family, and they called him 'Moss-Kit' because his father's by-name was 'Moss'.

Stone and nothing but stone at the quarry. A stone-dressing shed to the right-hand side, where the masons dressed stone in the winter, making inch-thick roofing slates in regular sizes, two-inch paving flags for house floors or pavements, and regular walling-stone, smooth as brick-work, in thicker gauges. Kit's father had spent nearly a year on one London order for square manhole flags with circular holes inset to take the iron manhole covers. He was a skilled man, Moss Calvert, and his white moustache bristled intently as he hand-worked the stone, but he was dead tired of cutting circles by the end. In the summer they worked outside on the dressing floor, where carts backed up to the dressed-stone banker to load. Then the shires would begin their long, shrieking downhill journey. Behind the dressing floor, beyond the forge, opened the black mouth of the drift, where raw stone was hewn underground and wheeled outside by a single pony dragging trucks over wooden rails.

On that hillside above Wensleydale, in green open country exposed to all the weathers of Yorkshire, this small quarry provided a living for half a village. Flagstones were sent by rail to pave London, walling stones and roofing slates went to build the mills and houses of Leeds and Bradford. The men, Moss Calvert among them, worked a ten-hour day, six till four, six days a week. They had Christmas Day and Good Friday as holidays without pay. Every Saturday evening Kit's father would come into the house and lay his wages on the table, eighteen shillings, less eighteenpence rent for a quarry house, leaving his mother with sixteen shillings and sixpence to provide for them.

Kit grew up with this knowledge as part of his understanding of the world and its interesting ways. Most of his friends and family lived as they did, happy enough with it, keeping their self-respect, ready to help others in times of need. Burtersett was a lively village, once a hamlet of scattered farms whose folk worked the valley meadows of Wensleydale and had sheep pasturing on the fells above. When Kit's grandparents came to work there the empty closes gradually filled with little rows of terraced cottages for the quarrymen slotted between the old, grey farms. Plenty of space remained for garden plots, hen runs, and the old barns were left stranded here and there alongside the houses. The crooked, narrow streets, not much more than built-up lanes, were called 'gates'. Highgate, Middlegate and Lowgate, an echo of the language of the Norse settlers who came to the Dales.

Kit explored the village regularly, being too active to keep still, knowing its every concern, from the one grocery shop to the barn loft where village 'balls' took place with the shires shaking their heads disapprovingly below. He began to stray into the fells above, beyond Yorburgh, Wether Fell and Ten End, where the wild country stretched into unknown Ribblesdale, coming back, late and ruddy, to tea and his mother's scolding. He knew the soft valley land below the village, the cattle pastures and hayfields beside the river Ure, and from the village he could look across the valley to Abbotside, the better lands that faced south and had once belonged to the Abbots of Jervaulx.

The village itself was full of friends and relatives, folk to turn to, or to learn from, by good or bad example. Just beyond the track to the quarry lived grandfather and grandmother Calvert with uncle Tom, the black sheep of the family. Uncle Tom could do no wrong in Grandma's eyes. When he was late bringing his load of beer back from Hawes, for there was no pub in the village, Grandma would get out her shawl and go to look for him. 'Sit down,'

53

snapped grandfather Calvert, 'sit down, let the beggar sleep out.' 'Nay,' said Grandma, a softness in her voice, still seeing her youngest as a baby, 'I don't blame him. You know how I like cockles; if he likes drink as well as I like cockles, I pity him.' Grandfather would shrug in disgust and turn back to the fire as she went out.

Once Uncle Tom took his prize hen over to a show at Muker in Swaledale. He won the class and was offered five pounds for the bird. Now five pounds was a good sum in those days, but Uncle Tom stubbornly refused the offer. 'Nay, she's that good, I'm going to show her in London.' He had a drink or two, then walked back over the tops to Hawes. He was hot when he got back, with a raging thirst, but he had no money left. So he took the hen from under his arm, wrung its neck, and exchanged the corpse for two pints of ale. That was Uncle Tom all through, and, though Kit had no respect for him, he enjoyed his company and the tales he told.

Now Uncle Rick was a more responsible man, and his wife, Aunt Nanny, a good housewife. They lived in a long cottage down Lowgate, the sort of house where you came in at the side of a little stone porch, found the kitchen and scullery in front of you, but took a dark, stone passage along the length of the building to reach the parlour. It was usually the kitchen for young Kit, and there, while the milk was giving, he would find Aunt Nanny making cheese, crumbly Wensleydale, rich from the fine grass of limestone pastures. She had four implements, a milk sieve, a tin, cheese kettle, bowls for crumbling the curd, and some wooden tubs for forming the cheese. The finished cheeses, like white grindstones, wept on wooden flakes in the scullery until they were mature. If you called on Aunt Nanny you always got a hunk of cheese to clutch and chew at, licking off the last crumbs from between your fingers.

It was a short cut back home from Uncle Rick's to their own cottage at the top of the village, next to an old hay barn and opposite the field for the quarry horses. An ordinary cottage, with kitchen and parlour, two bedrooms over, one for mother and father, the other for Kit and

54

Bob. Behind was a small yard with the privy in it. Sometimes grandfather Fothergill, his mother's old dad, would come to dinner, with bowler hat and walking stick. Grandfather Fothergill was a kindly man, even though he always had a puzzled frown, and he had a halo of white whiskers round his wide chin. After supper he would sit Kit comfortably between his legs in front of the fire, a clog on each side to hold him firm, and push his bowler to the back of his head. Kit could see the white scroll patterns his mother had made round the edge of the scrubbed hearth-stone. 'Now, Kit,' grandfather Fothergill would say, 'look at yon boiler.' This was the cast-iron, hot-water boiler beside the fire with its raised circular plaque for the maker's name. 'Now, tell us what's on the top line.' 'B.' 'What's "B" stand for?' 'Bob.' 'Right, what's next?' 'O.' 'And what's "O" stand for?' 'Orange.' 'Next?' 'R.' 'What's that stand for?' 'Robert.' 'Nay, you've said that already.' And so it went on until Kit had spelled out the whole 'BOWERBANK. IRONMONGERS. PENRITH'. Kit took to his letters like a lamb to the teat and he never forgot that boiler front. It lives in his memory to this day.

Soon enough it was time for school, time to leave the village every morning and walk the dusty road to Hawes, to the town, with its shops, market square, bustle of carts, cattle, horses and people, the metropolis of his experience. Kit reached school, lunch bag over his shoulder, heavy with its inevitable double jam sandwiches and half a bannock. At lunch time they were turned out of school, and in winter it was either the joiner's shop where they were periodically driven out for heaping too many shavings on the fire, or else the cold seat of the outside lavatories. Sometimes they could beg a bit of good meat or a pasty from young Jimmy, who was thin, weak and consumptive, and whose mother had to tempt him to eat. No such trouble with Kit, or with Bob when he followed on to school.

A man they called Farding Dick lived in Hawes and looked after cattle that were being shipped to Liverpool. Sometimes they had a bit of milk in them, and he didn't want it, so he would skim the cream for butter. Then fat old Farding Dick's wife would come to the corner of the bridge on the road to Burtersett and stop Kit on his way back from school. 'Tell thy mam to send a can down, and a ha'penny, for some blue milk.' Kit would tell his mother and be sent off next day with a six-pint can. They used to carry the full can back in turn, but one day they couldn't agree, Kit said it was Bob's turn and Bob said it wasn't. Kit didn't dare leave the can behind, but once they were out of the town he put it down in the middle of the road. 'It's thy turn,' he said. 'No it ain't.' 'It's thy turn, and thou'll carry it . . . or I'll fight thee for it.' 'Right,' said Bob, 'I'll fight thee.' So all the Burtersett lads and lassies made a ring, and the two brothers squared off at each other. But Kit never even got a blow in. Bob took one shot and hit Kit square on the nose. It burst. Blood flew everywhere and Kit howled. Bob and the other children ran off to Burtersett leaving Kit bawling and bleeding beside the can. He had to carry it home alone. That was Kit's only fight, and he lost it, but he still tells the tale.

His mother was always careful and every halfpenny had to count. Even at Christmas time, when father had a day's leave, he would take the lads along for a stint of muck-spreading before it was quite dark. At a halfpenny a heap they need only rake out seventy-two heaps to make up the three shillings that were cut from father's wages on account of Christmas Day. And on New Year's morning the lads were sent out at six o'clock, dressed in their best and equipped with a pillowcase and a purse, to go begging gifts from house to house. 'Now then,' said mother, 'put any money in t'purse . . . apples and oranges go into t'pillowcase.' 'What if they give us parkin?' 'Ay, well,' answered mother carefully, 'tha can eat t'parkin . . . but don't go asking for it!' So they went the rounds and came home and the garnering were counted; two shillings and eightpence in the purse. That would be put to the clothing club in Hawes, and maybe by sale-time in March they might have enough for a pair of blue cord trousers apiece.

The apples and oranges meant apple pies and marmalade at the dead time of the year.

Any unusual expenditure took long deliberation and sometimes a good deal of argument. His father would look at Kit, labouring intently over his homework, and say, 'I don't know what's wrong with that lad of mine, our Kit. He's got books and books, and he's always after another. I've never had a book in my life, and I don't intend to.' But none of those books belonged to Kit himself, they were all from school, or borrowed, and Kit was nine, and had set his heart on one particular book. It was a *Collins Pronouncing Dictionary*, displayed in the bookshop window in Hawes. It had illustrations, woodcuts, black and intriguing, of seals, herons, ferns, doves and dovetails. That book was a mine of fascinating information, even down to the 'Directions for commencing and addressing letters to persons of rank': dukes, lords, and such, though Kit didn't really suspect he was likely to need it. He would read anything that was in print. So Kit went on at his Dad, only to get the regular reply, 'I don't know what he wants with it.' Until one day, leaning over the kitchen table, Dad asked mother for a couple of shillings and said he was taking Kit down to Hawes. 'You'll have to come down wi' me. I don't know what tha' wants.' That was all, but Kit got his dictionary.

That was sheer extravagance, and Kit was more often making the savings, or helping where he could. When mother wanted to give father a treat on a Saturday evening she would send Kit off to the butchers for a sheep's head. They were threepence 'with eyes' and fourpence without, so Kit always bought them 'with eyes' and skinned them himself. It saved a penny. Then they would boil it over Friday night in a big pan hanging on a reckon-hook over the fire, and leave it to cool. For a really tasty dish, mother would take out the brains and mash them with butter, salt and pepper. Then, when father came home from work, they would all sit round the fire, eating the paste on bread toasted at the bars, with good, hot mugs of tea to wash it down.

Laiking

'Well', said Kit's father to his mother as he came into the kitchen from the quarry, 'that's the end of that!' She looked at his face for a minute. 'What's the matter?' 'If I'm not worth a pound a week I won't go onto that hill again.' 'Well what can we do?' Father banged his tea bottle down on the table. 'I'll buy a tin whistle and go blowing it up and down the dale till they have to give me summat just to get rid of me before I go back there for eighteen shilling!'

The quarry owner, Mr Johnson, had stopped behind to sort out the rest of the men, those who had given in and would still take eighteen shillings. Now he marched down from the quarry and straight into the house. Since he also owned the house he never thought of knocking. 'Art thou going up onto that hill on Monday morning?' Father answered slowly. 'No . . . only for a pound a week.' 'It's eighteen shillings, same as t'others.' 'No!' 'Well, if that's final, you're out of this house next week – and if you don't get out, you'll be put out.' Mr Johnson had married into the quarry family, he had expensive tastes, owned a trotting horse and carriage and was not to be won over by sentiment for old and trusted workers. He turned and walked away without another word. Mother stood there shaking, suddenly left without wages or home, thrown out into the world like a naked child. It was 1916, two years into a war. Father sat down. He had a wife and two boys to provide for and all he knew was working stone. What was he to do?

Oddly enough, the war came to the rescue of Kit's threatened family. That very day the yardman at the Hawes auction mart had left his job and taken work at another quarry. He did it in fear of the trenches, for conscription was to be brought in for men in 'inessential' jobs, and he couldn't see that an auction yardman's work was essential, at least when he was a bachelor. The chairman of the

58

auction mart lived in Burtersett, and now he needed a yardman at once, for the next auction day. Moss Calvert had a good name for himself, and was known in the village to be a capable man with beasts, so the chairman sought him out. 'You're out of a job, Moss, dost' fancy taking on at t'cattle mart?' Moss raised his eyebrows, for here was manna from heaven. He took the job, and at the same time the chairman found them a house down Middlegate. In one swift week their lives, fortunes and home had changed dramatically. For ten-year-old Kit it took some beating.

Surprising complications followed, as father's earnings fluctuated with the auction work, but gradually rose above the pound a week level. Mother couldn't stop her saving habits, not after all those careful years, and one evening Kit overheard a conversation as he sat at his homework. 'It's ten pound now,' she said, 'and I can't sleep over it, I can hardly leave the house in case someone takes it. Billy Jack says I ought to put it in t'bank.' Father roared at this. 'I want nowt wi' banks!' 'Ah, but it's safe in t'bank, and I'm worried to death by it where it is.' So Kit's father made his economic philosophy quite clear. 'If it's worrying thee, then get the damn thing spent. I reckon nowt to banks if I can't look after me own brass. I don't want no banks!'

There was certainly no way that Kit's mother could relax the eternal search for cash or kind. Kit had part-time jobs as soon as he was capable. He began by helping the butcher in the village, bringing water to the lowing beasts in the hunger-house behind his shop, where they starved for a day before being slaughtered. He learnt the mysteries of cutting up the livers into two and three penn'orths for the traditional Thursday night dish. Then, when he was eleven, he was taken on at the Queen's Hotel in Hawes, to work Saturdays for fourpence and his keep. Odd jobs, sweeping up, chopping wood, clearing-out cellars, kept him busy. Kit hated it. He didn't mind the beasts, he could get on with them, but he couldn't bear the housework. Kit was a proud lad, in his way, with his wits about him, and seeing what had nearly happened to father, he vowed that one day he would be his own boss.

So it was a question of what to do when he was twelve and schooling was over. The quarry was out. Father wouldn't let him go there, and in any case Mr Johnson was rapidly going downhill to bankruptcy after an expensive law suit over mining rights. In Burtersett it was either the quarry or farming, and if you went into farming the important thing was to get your feet under someone else's table. Given board and lodging as a farmer's lad, the wages were secondary. So Kit got taken on at Lowgate Farm, just below his home. It was an old farmhouse, sitting at the end of Lowgate, with scattered fields, some thirty acres of meadow in the bottoms, about sixty acres of higher pasture, a farm run in the traditional way, with a small laithe, or barn, for each group of about half a dozen dairy cattle. The cattle lived in the fields close by, or wintered in the laithe. The muck was stored beside the laithe, and some fields were kept for hay, the fodder then going into the hayloft for winter use.

It was an efficient system for that rough, open country-side, but required someone to be constantly at work, from laithe to laithe, seeing to the cattle, milking, collecting the milk and bringing it home to the farm. That was Kit's job. Old Ralph Waggett and his wife were over seventy, and the only other person in the house was his last, unmarried daughter, Alice. Ralph had been a lead miner in Swaledale most of his life, had scratted money up until he could buy a small farm, but by then he had the miner's cough, and damaged lungs. So Kit learnt all a dairy farmer's work, spreading muck, fencing off with dry stone walls, milking, caring for the beasts. The one thing he couldn't manage was mowing hay, he could use a scythe for five minutes, but when it came to sharpening his blade he always left it blunt as the backside of a rake.

When he was twelve, and just starting, the hardest job of all was bringing back the milk from the high pastures after milking. He had a tin back-can that would hold seven gallons, and, what with the weight of the milk, the straps cutting into his shoulders, and the rough ground, it was all he could do to carry it the distance and edge it through the last two stiles before he reached the road and Burtersett. When there was really too much milk to carry, then Mr Waggett let him take the donkey, with a back-can on each side. If he gave it more than ten gallons to carry it wouldn't get up to go home. You might kick it, beat it, call it every name under the sun, but it wouldn't budge. But Kit had a way with beasts and he soon learnt the donkey's secret. The creature was a secret tobacco chewer! So Kit bought an ounce of twist tobacco for threepence halfpenny, which is how he learnt to smoke himself, and bit off a piece. Then he held it out, 'Get up, Jack,' the donkey looked sideways. 'Come on, Jack,' and he pushed it towards the flaring nostrils. When Jack got the scent of tobacco he made for it with his yellow teeth. But Kit was too quick. He drew back and up came the donkey. Jack would take the tobacco from Kit's fingers and suck away at it until both of them landed home with the milk.

Kit came to prefer a clay pipe after some experimental tobacco chewing in his teens. The donkey was more set in his ways. One evening while he and Jack were still new acquaintances, he brought the milk home at half-past seven. It was May, still light and sunny, he hadn't been long at work and he could see all his friends going off to play. So he turned Jack into the paddock and set off after them. But a hasty rap on the farmhouse window summoned him before he got far. 'Hey,' said Ralph Waggett in his breathless way, 'where's t'going?' 'I'm going to laik.' 'Just going to laik, eh? Can't tha find nowt else to do but laik?' Kit looked round at the sunlit fields. 'I've put t'milk in, I've put donkey in, I've put all t'gear in. I don't think there's nowt else to do.' 'I'd better find thee summat, then.' So Mr Waggett came out of the parlour and paddled Kit round to the paddock where the donkey stood. 'Do you see all them dockins and dog-standards,' said Mr Waggett, pointing to the weeds, 'pull 'em till supper time . . . Then tha can come out and laik.' He coughed, twice, and went back inside. Kit stood in the paddock and looked at the donkey, and the donkey looked at him. The evening sun shone golden across the wide valley and he could hear his mates' shouts from the riverside. 'I don't know whether thee or me is daftest,' was all he could say as he bent to take hold of the first dock leaves. Jack went on chewing, with a contented look in his eye.

Nevertheless, there were times when Kit slipped the collar, evaded Mr Waggett's watchful eye, and went out laiking all the same. Burtersett lads had some odd customs, such as going pace-egging in November rather than Easter, and without taking any eggs with them. But they still came out of the darkness towards the lamplit windows of their neighbours, hooting and hallooing and singing their song – 'Here's one or two jolly boys all in a line, we've come a pace-egging, it's pace-egging time!' Kit got his friends some of the rudd that Mr Waggett used to mark his rams at tupping time and they reddened their faces well. 'Lord Nelson' had a fine star cut out of a blacking-tin lid, and they came down Lowgate making a tremendous din with their song until they beat on Uncle Rich's door.

Uncle Rich had heard the din as he sat in the parlour, so he said to his daughter, 'Maggie, here come them pace-eggers, lass. Quick! Hide thisen behind t'door . . . and when they've come into t'passage, lock it behind 'em!' Well, Kit and his mates came yelling in, right down the passage, and they banged open the parlour door. There stood Uncle Rich in the lamplight, with the blunderbuss from over the mantel in his hands and aimed right at them, and a furious scowl on his face. 'I've seen thee,' he said. 'Get out! Get going . . . or I'll shoot thee,' and he made to cock the gun. Kit recoiled, so did his mates. They rushed back down the passage, crashed into the door, fell over each other in heaps in the darkness. Every time they looked along the passage they could see Uncle Rich's scowling face above the muzzle of the gun. They scrambled over each other, back and forth, losing medals and begging baskets, until so exhausted that they subsided into a miserable heap on the floor. Uncle Rich's scowl was beginning to break down at the sight. It was more than flesh and blood could bear. At last Maggie opened the door and let them escape, all their pace-egging ardour over for that year. Uncle Rich sat down in the parlour to laugh till he cried.

When Kit first went to work for Ralph Waggett his mother had said, 'Just mind and behave thiself. When tha's sitting at table, just remember, if they offer thee a bit of pasty, say, and tha likes it. Then say, "Yes, please." But if they offer summat else after that, then say "No thank you." Don't take two pieces . . . One's plenty!' Now one day Kit was at supper with the Waggetts and they offered him a tomato. He'd never tasted a tomato in his life. He was tempted, sorely, but shook his head and said, 'No thank you.' 'Are t'sure tha won't take one, Kit?' 'No, thank you.' His mouth was watering for that tomato, but he remembered what his mother had said. If he did have a tomato then he couldn't have that heel of loaf, and there was more substance for the belly in that loaf than in all the strange, fruity taste of a tomato. He was sure of it. So young Kit bided his time, and got what he wanted. It was a lesson he taught himself, not to hanker after strange new things but to go for what could be done. He could manage well enough, Wensleydale fashion.

Kit worked for Ralph Waggett for two and a half years. He started with five shillings a week wages, getting sixpence extra every half year, until when he was fourteen and a half, and getting seven shillings, he asked Mr Waggett to put it up to eight directly. Kit reckoned he was worth that much to the farm. But the Waggetts said they couldn't afford it, not an extra sixpence a week, that was over a pound a year. So Kit took himself off to the hirings at market day in Hawes. He knew his own worth and wasn't married, and, if nothing came of it, he could always swallow his pride a little and go back to the Waggetts for seven shillings and sixpence, plus his board. He stood there in the old market place, waiting like the other out of work labourers (some boys like himself, others grown men with families, or white-haired grandfathers), waiting beside the cattle, patiently waiting to see if they might be taken on. Kit had determined to try hard to get ten shillings a week now he'd been forced to it. That would be a real triumph. One or two farmers nodded at him but passed by. He wasn't their kind of beast.

After a while a sharpish-looking man, fairly small, but wearing a natty blue suit, a billycock hat on his head, perched very jaunty, and a bamboo switch under his arm, came over. Kit knew him as a cattle-dealer from Bainbridge, further down the Dale. The man said, 'Art t'hiring?' 'Yes.' 'Work for me?' 'Aye, if you'll give me plenty.' Moses Atkinson looked him over again, nodded, and said in a loud voice so that all around could hear. 'I'll give thee a pound a week.' Kit could have dropped under the pavings, but he wasn't going to wait for the man to change his mind. 'Aye,' he said, 'I'll come.'

A Good Master

Kit had his foot under Moses Atkinson's table directly and set about learning the trade of cattle-dealer. A year at that job made a lad acquainted with more beasts than a lifetime of small farming, and it was knowledge that might be put to good use. He was rising fifteen and it was time to begin thinking how he might get on. Meanwhile it could do no harm to migrate the four miles to Bainbridge, live with Moses, get paid a pound a week and learn.

Mind you, Moses was not the sort of master you could respect. He had risen fast, and without ballast, son of Will Atkinson, who had two wives and twenty-four children, but little else to bless him with. Most of the family became dull, slogging, farmer's men, but Moses was shrewder. He got started in cattle-dealing just before the war began in 1914. Prices rose remorselessly. He bought from farmers or at market in Hawes or Northallerton, and always sold at a profit. He spent his gains freely, liked his drink, bought

64

a few rounds and, to give him his due, paid his staff well, though that was partly a show for the watching neighbours who couldn't really accept his good fortune. Moses walked through Bainbridge with bamboo stick and billycock as if he were mayor of the town.

Kit was taken on just as the war was ending and Moses was at his busiest. He had work enough to do, collecting cattle from the farms, dashing to market or to the station, tending them, cleaning up and polishing them a bit for market. A shining coat, well-soaped, a well-waxed horn, good bags rudded a bit with rouge, these sold a doubtful cow then, as now. Kit learnt to know a good beast underneath the soap and wax. He also had to learn to deal with those that fell sick. Young stock would get husk. You would see them standing, necks stretched out, coughing, choking and retching, not able to eat properly. They would cough and cough, until at last, out came a wriggling knot of the little parasitic worms that had lodged in their windpipes, mixed up with mucus in a slimy mess, landing on the grass. Then along would come other cattle, eat the grass, and off they would start. All of them would soon be coughing, like to weaken and lose their value.

At first Kit was told to try the smoke treatment for this. He would light a small fire, burn sulphur on it, so that a thick, choking, yellow smoke billowed out. Then, with the yardman holding each beast in turn, Kit would take blow-bellows, fill them with smoke and puff it down the animal's throat. They fairly struggled at it, and sneezed, making as much fuss as if they were being slaughtered on the spot. If the smoke didn't work, and often it didn't, the only remedy was to send for Dick Bell, the old cow doctor. He had a range of secret recipes, usually vile, black and sticky, containing a fair proportion of tar, sulphur and turpentine. One of these was reported good for the husk, and Dick would slowly ladle it into each affected beast through a funnel made out of a large cow's horn. If they were strong beasts most of them recovered from both disease and remedy.

With a job so various as cattle-dealing Kit also found

time for a fair amount of laiking. He was a quick lad, with a sense of fun, not likely to turn into a sober adult too early. Now for some reason the postman in Bainbridge was a target for the boys, perhaps because he always rose to the occasion and was full of fireworks for a while, though his anger generally fizzled out without too much damage in the way of consequences. The postman had a pig, a well-fleshed sow he was proud of, and he kept her in an old earth-closet behind the house. So, one night when he was sitting outside the pub, and the lads were hanging about, getting on his nerves a bit, and he had been telling them to clear off, Kit said to him, 'You want to watch out, you know, George, or you'll be losing that sow.' He rose at that one. 'Nobody can get at my sow. She's locked in . . . so don't you lads think owt of laikin about with her!'

That was just what Kit wanted him to say, because they knew that the closet door was padlocked at night, but they also knew that the cleaning-out hole still existed at the back, and they reckoned that they could just squeeze that fat sow out through it if they could move the stone slab that blocked it. Later that night the conspirators gathered, and, with much noisy hushing of each other, made their way to the back of the closet. Silent heaves, punctuated by pauses for heavy breathing, the alarmed wait after what sounded like a window opening in the house, these all followed. At last they had the stone shifted and managed to get the sow out and ride her away. It took some doing, because she weighed about ten stone, didn't really want to go out into the dark, and was inclined to grunt loudly under her master's window, even though they had a noose of rope around her snout.

But that on its own was not enough. It was too obvious, not witty enough for Kit and his friends. So they went down the town to the house of an old gentleman, a quiet, simple soul, who never locked his sty, and removed his new little pig that was only about eight weeks old. They left him the postman's sow in exchange. Then they carried the little piglet back to the postman's. It was an easier job than riding the sow. They pushed it through the hole, shoved the stone back, hid all traces of their work, and waited impatiently for morning.

Such a commotion followed, for George always rose to the occasion and once he had unlocked the closet in the morning and stared goggle-eyed at his sow's transformation, he was a walking advertisement for his woes. A sensible man would have kept quiet, waited, and thought it over. But no, he roamed the streets, questioning all and sundry, at one moment suspecting the publican, who had taken some pigs to the station that morning, at another even Moses Atkinson, who wasn't above dealing in the odd pig or two. Kit kept out of sight when George came round the corner. Well, the post was late that day, but in the evening all pig-owners tended to gather at the local creamery, where they used the curds for cheese and sold off the whey. Kit was there, and so was George and along came the old gentleman with his innocent face. The dairyman said, 'You'll want your gallon of milk for your pig?' 'Well,' he said, 'I don't know. I think I'd better have two gallons. My pig's grown tremendously since last night. I don't know what's happened, but I've quite a fine pig today and I'm sure it'll drink more than a gallon.' Well this was too much for Kit. He began to splutter and choke until at last he could hold it no longer. He had to laugh out loud or die. George saw him, and, ever suspicious, jumped to conclusions. The right ones this time. He also jumped on Kit and would have throttled him if the men there hadn't stopped him. So the sow went back home and George was a little quieter for a while. So was Kit.

Kit had also a good deal of running about to do after Moses. His boss would say, 'I'm off up to Countersett,' this was a village back into the hills, 'get trap out. Tha can drive me there. Old Sam's selling up his pub . . . There'll be free beer, and I might see summat I fancy at auction . . . I've a mind to a cigar or two.' This would be a whole day away from work. 'What about t'beasts,' said Kit, 'there's some as needs milking.' 'Oh, ay,' said Moses, 'tha can allus go back for t'milking. But mind you get to Countersett before they close-up. I'm not walking home.' So Kit harnessed up the old mare, drove Moses to Countersett, left him soaking well in the beer, and went back to the beasts that were his charge.

Later, as it was growing dark, and the western sun shone down the Dale, he took the old mare quietly back up the steep, winding road to Countersett and tied her up outside the pub. The sale was over, bits and pieces of old equipment, barrels, tubs, crates, broken chairs stood in desolate heaps outside. But the lamplit noise still echoed out into the road from the stripped out bar. Nothing much remained inside but a long, fixed, wooden settle against the wall, a few declining barrels, half crates of unsold bottles and a half bar top. Moses was holding court with his cronies against the bar.

Kit was just about to go over to Moses and announce his presence when a sharp female voice called out behind him. 'Where is he? Where's the beggar?' The woman's clogs tapped brusquely on paving slabs outside the threshold, but she couldn't yet see inside. At that moment a rather portly, white-haired but distinctly unsteady farmer was seen to dive full-length under the settle, cracking his head painfully on the underside of the seat as he went. Quite instinctively, the five comfortable gentlemen on the seat drew their legs upright, closed their knees in ordered ranks and fenced him completely from view. A look of nervous conspiracy spread over their fuddled faces.

The farmer's housekeeper paused, scornfully, on the threshold and looked round at this scene of masculine enjoyment. 'Where is he?', she repeated. 'Gone,' came the chorus. 'No he's not! Beggar's never come home.' She looked suspiciously at the seated cherubs. 'He's somewhere hereabouts! Where have you hidden him?' 'No, he's not here,' came the instant response. A brief pause in the ceremony left the room in silence. She looked round again. Now whether it was the drink, or the blow to his head, the farmer was in no good shape to tell, but from under the settle, behind the hedge of knees, came a dreadful groan. It was followed by a heartrending retching. The house-keeper's look sharpened. 'I can hear the beggar . . . He's under there.' Like a sensible drover, she had her stick already with her, a good knobbly-ended blackthorn, and she rapped a hearty tune along the shins of the chorus-line. They swung aside, up and down, with cries of pain, to reveal the wretched farmer sprawling in sand and dust. She hauled him out sack-like, poked and prodded him to his feet, to be driven home, groaning all the way. Her sweet encouragements could be heard above his lowings long after they had vanished into the darkness.

How Moses laughed. 'Come on over, Kit,' he said, noticing his man, 'have some beer. Dids't see yon slave-driver?' 'Aye.' 'Have a drink, then,' and Moses poured another round from the jug. In the end there were only a few of them left. Moses had offered a lift to old Toff, who had drunk so much by now that he had a shivering fit, and was calling out 'Watter . . . watter . . . get me some watter.' So Moses kept selling him the last four bottles of lemonade, 'It's better than watter – drink up lad,' rattling the marbles in the empty bottles and winking at Kit as he got rid of the last of Sam's stock. At last the beer ran out and Kit was able to bundle Toff into the back of the cart. Moses climbed up beside him and lit one of his newly acquired cigars.

They set off into the darkness, down the winding road, Kit straining his eyes to make out the way from the white gleam of the limestone surface. Moses was carolling away and puffing at his cigar alternately. The glowing end describing complicated circles in the air as he conducted whilst he sang. Then Moses began to lose patience with their slow, careful pace. Kit didn't know the road that well and he reckoned they could do without going over the edge. The drop was nasty in places. 'Get on, you old beggar, get on!' Moses shouted at the mare. Leaning forward suddenly he prodded the horse's rump with his cigar. She lurched off, whinnying and kicking, throwing the trap from side to side. It was all Kit could do to hold onto the reins. The road was narrow, stone-walled on either side, and yet Moses kept doing it, then singing, then prodding the horse again. 'Get on, you old beggar, get on!'

It was only thanks to providence, and meeting no-one else on the way, that they reached Bainbridge alive and undamaged.

Kit could see such a smash-up in prospect for Moses, if not today, then in a month or two. Apart from the pay he had nothing to gain from such a master. The war was over, prices were falling, and profits didn't come easily. Yet Moses still spent money like lemonade. Only the week before they'd had one cow driven back and forth from market to market until it was so knocked up it sold for a quarter less than Moses had paid for it. That was not good business. It was time to look around and move on. Time for Kit to find himself a good master. He was known and respected by now, not just an untrained lad, and he'd met a fair number of farmers through the cattle-dealing.

So Kit was quickly taken on by Mr James Scarr of Coleby Hall, leaving Moses to prod away with his bamboo cane for a little longer, until the crash came and he ended his days as a carter for the council. Kit was more far-seeing than most young farmworkers. Coleby Hall was something more permanent, more traditional. Set across the Dale from Bainbridge, in Lower Abbotside, it was a fine, seventeenth-century house with the land to go with it, and sheep gaits on the moor for nigh on four hundred sheep. That would be Kit's main job, to shepherd. Something new to learn, for though he was not a stranger to sheep, most of his work had been with cattle. Now in his late teens, a good, strong, intelligent worker, he was worth the sixty pounds a year that Mr Scarr offered him.

James Scarr was a good master. A proper squire, active about the farm in his tweed jacket, breeches and soft trilby hat. A human man to the farmhands who shared his table. It was Kit's delight to get the boss out walking with them. All you had to do, then, was say 'I saw a couple o'trout in your beck t'other day . . . Just yonder.' 'Did you Kit, where was that?' 'Oh, just over yonder.' They'd have to go to look. Soon Mr Scarr would be flat on his belly beside them, peering into the swirling stream, and the morning would vanish in gubbling trout. That was how to be with

70

a master. Next day you'd work even harder for it, and he knew good work when he saw it. Kit reckoned he could stay with Mr Scarr all his life.

As a hobby Mr Scarr used to shape and carve walking sticks. Nothing could beat his joy when he found a perfect hazel shoot with the right knob of root on the end and could sit down by the fire to whittle it into a grand fit for his hand, with perhaps an incised band or two for decoration. Then he would proudly display the finished stick, well-oiled and gleaming, to his family and men. Young Kit decided to try his hand at this himself and show the boss what he could do. So he went up the ghyll behind the farm and, after some searching, found a beautiful shoot, growing at an angle to the root. Just right. He took his axe and began to hack it out. Not being skilled at the job, he nicked it in the wrong place and when he came to heave it up the head broke off, leaving just a lumpy outcrop on the end. Disgusted, but still not willing to give up, Kit took it home and worked at it as best he could.

Then one evening a week or two later, Mr Scarr came over to Kit after supper in the kitchen. 'Has t'been up in the wood, Kit?' 'Aye, once or twice.' 'You know that tree about at the top, to the right hand of beck corner!' 'Aye!' 'Didst get a stick out of there?' 'Aye.' 'Well, you bullock-head . . . that's a stick I've been waiting two years to take . . . that one. It's the best bit I've seen in years.' He grunted, half angry at the thought. Then he asked Kit, 'Well, let's see what sort of stick you've got out of it. By what's left I reckon you made a right mess.' Shamefaced, Kit admitted, 'Well . . . I have rather.' 'Let's have a look.' So Kit brought the stick, and Mr Scarr gazed in amazement at this ruin, descending into his broadest tongue at the sight. 'Why . . . thou calf-head . . . th'art fit for nowt . . . get on out and take it with thee. It grieves me to see it!' He was more taken up by that stick than by the loss of a sheep.

But that grief was soon forgotten, and the regular work of the farm continued. Kit was busy at every job, from milking to haymaking, except of course, the mowing. He also increased his knowledge of sick beasts, learning the strange, archaic practice of rowelling. When a cow was thin of flesh, dull of eye, its hair bristly and matted, and no obvious sickness ailed it, then Kit would shake his head at it and say, 'Tha wants a good rowelling.' He would tie the beast securely to the boskins in the laithe. Then, with a sharp knife he made a good wide cut into the dewlap. 'Whoa there, hold steady lass.' Working his hand round inside he freed the skin from the flesh, feeling the warmth of the living beast as he tugged at her soft tissue. So he created a pocket, a hollow inside her neck which was filled with an irritant salve composed principally of grease and turpentine smeared onto a folded packet of stinging nettles. That stage of the treatment ended with a cord tied through the double hole in the dewlap and securely knotted in a loop. 'That's right lass,' he would say as he calmed her, 'it's for thy good,' and the cow would shake her head indignantly at the cruelty of it all, her eyes still rolling a little, before she settled. Kit would leave this ingenious cure to do its work for a day or two, giving time for all the badness in the cow's body, the felon, to gather to the irritant and fill the pocket. But each day he went to the cow and pulled the cord, sliding it to and fro in its hole so as to prevent the wound from healing. The beast came to expect some pain and might go for him with horn or hoof, so he generally kept her tied up in the laithe while he was rowelling. She would certainly bawl a bit when he pulled the cord, but, again, Kit knew what to say, 'Whoa there, old girl, it's for thy good!' Then, when the matter had gathered, he'd press the abscess between his thumbs and out would blurt all the felon, foul-smelling, best away. Once it was all over it was wonderful how she'd pick-up. No doubt about it, rowelling worked, it was one of a skilled cowman's best tricks.

Kit also had the sheep to care for, a dog to handle and all a shepherd's tasks. Just as it was his job to heal the cattle, so he was also called on to treat the young rams, breaking the frontal bone with his knuckle as he held each struggling beast between his knees. A sharp rap, feel the bone go, then break away the loose pieces with his thumb, and it was done. You could feel the hollow in the forehead ever after. They called it scauping, though why it was always done he never knew. But working the sheep also kept him long days on the moor far from the farm. One winter his job became much worse because the sheep gaits in Upper Abbotside were bought out by a shooting syndicate and not grazed, the grouse having priority. Since it was unfenced moor, the lower Abbotside sheep naturally spread over the whole area, miles beyond their normal range, and as far as the Buttertubs pass.

Then the bad weather came, heavy snow, and the sheep must be got in. Kit walked up from Coleby Hall with the dog. It was snowing solidly, but he soon grew warm in his army greatcoat and so he loosed it to cool off. On the moor top a blizzard was driving, icy, heavy, hiding the world, and he still had the sheep to sort out. It was bitter cold by now and he made to fasten his coat. But his hands were frozen, and the cloth around the buttonholes was so stiff he couldn't twist a single button through. So he took out his knife, cut the buttonholes larger, and happily slipped the buttons through.

Kit spent several hours roaming the length of the moor, gathering in a flock of nigh two hundred sheep, and at the far end he at last turned for home. They would do well to get back before dark at that pace and in that weather. As he turned into the wind, the first gust tore his coat wide open. He could find no way to fasten it again, so in the end he set himself to plod into the driving snow. He froze as he went. The wet snow built up in freezing layers against his chest and belly, working its way around his back. Heavier and heavier became the effort of moving forward. He could barely see the sheep. The dog kept by his side. No-one knew where he was, for he could be anywhere on the moor and it might take days to find him. He was never nearer to giving up than on that day. All he wanted to do was lie down, to stop struggling, not to fight, but lie down and sleep. One step, then another, that was all he could manage, just aware that the sheep followed. Never ending, it seemed, his feet and the dog finding the way, until, at last, he found himself back at Coleby Hall, black against the snow, and the sheep with him, of course, the sheep he had been sent for.

Those were really five good years of work, when Kit became a grown man and could tackle anything on the farm. As he said, he might be there yet, he was happy enough. But one evening a friend was taking him pillion on a motorbike along the road from Bainbridge to Hawes, going to a dance. The road was narrow, stone-walled as always, and round a bend they came upon a drunken farmer galloping his milk-float down the middle of the road. It was a terrifying sight, like a war chariot, all shouts, hooves and rumbling wheels. The bike swerved wildly to avoid it. Kit's foot swung off the footrest in the violence of the manoeuvre. Smash went his knee against the iron hub of the milk-float wheel. He was off the bike, lying in the road in a roaring pain, the milk-float gone on its devastating way. Kit's right leg lay at all angles, broken to pieces, and the world rose and sank around him in sharp agony followed by unconsciousness.

Wensleydale Cheese

Kit had to be taken to Leeds Infirmary after his accident, and they kept him in for ten weeks until his leg was put together. The cart wheel appears to have survived unscathed. Then, of course, he was unfit for proper farmwork for several months. Whilst he recovered, Kit's father gave him odd jobs around Hawes auction mart. Moss Calvert's move from the quarry had proved a great success, and by this time, 1924, when Kit was twenty-one, Moss had risen to be yard manager on a salary of two hundred and fifty pounds a year. That was real security for Kit's mother, she could save in earnest without the worry of seeing her savings spent. Kit, with some of this tradition in him, was beginning to think what he could do with his smashed career and growing tired of odd jobs. He wasn't a man to brood, but he wanted to be doing.

On Mayday it was customary for farmers and their men to renew contracts for another year, or else to agree to part. Kit would have known the horseman who rode into the auction yard, the Mayday after his accident, at the far end of a moor. 'Good morning, Mr Scarr.' 'Hello, Kit. I came to ask if you were coming back?' He scratched his head. It was tempting, but Kit didn't think he would always be a farmer's man. And the break had been made for him. 'Well, I don't know . . . you see, I've got a sort of a job now, and you've got a man.' Kit somehow had never completely thought out in his own mind whether he wanted to go back. He had enjoyed the life, no doubt about it, but now he'd become used to the free-wheeling ways of the mart. He had to make up his mind. 'You've taken on yon lad from Askrigg.' 'Aye, but I only took him on temporary. He knows it's your job.' Kit, with time to think, suddenly knew to a certainty that he didn't want to go back to the old ways. There was a streak of independence in him. He wasn't made to be a servant all his days. 'Well, I don't know,' he answered slowly, for this was the crunch, a good job going, 'I don't like pushing the lad out.' Then in a rush to get the decision over. 'If you're satisfied, Mr Scarr, then carry on.' They shook hands with due respect and Mr Scarr rode off.

Afterwards Kit looked at his prospects and wondered. How far would helping out at the auction mart get him, even with his father as yard manager? But when he saw his chances, Kit took them. He began dealing in cattle in a very small way, taking the odd calf from farmers who had had a cow serviced for the milk and found the calf, though necessary, a nuisance. It was slow progress, scraping up pounds from pence, slapping hands over a deal and giving back one of the precious shillings as luck money. Time, native shrewdness, and not rushing into big risks like Moses, began to produce their rewards. Kit rented a four acre field to hold his stock. Then, after a while, as he says himself, he was rash and got himself a wife.

Now, with responsibilities beyond his own living, and the prospect of more to follow, inevitable as the farmer's calf, he had to find steadier prospects, but he was set on being his own master. There would be no return to service. So he rented a little farm, sixty acres in all, though not such a farm as storybooks picture. It was the most untidy set-up you could imagine. His farmhouse was a cottage on the outskirts of Hawes, his fields scattered here, there and everywhere. It was difficult to run, inefficient, and hard work. But it was his own while he paid the rent. And it was not all disadvantages, for the situation of the house meant that people came from the bottom end of town to buy milk direct, and that was a help to their income. Also his brother Bob joined him to work the place, and Bob had turned into a sturdy, regular farmworker.

It was hard, but healthy work, running a small farm like that, with traditional equipment, house, brother and wife. It was a while before Kit would even afford a windrowing machine which the horse could tow along after the mowers, to toss the hay and lay in regular rows for gathering. His father came that evening to help load the hay onto the sledge for the horse to drag it to the laithe. Kit's fields were mostly too steep for wheels, and, in any case, a hay sledge was a great deal cheaper than a cart. They set off across the field, bend and lift, laying an armful of hay in turn onto the sledge, with the horse moving slowly in time to their actions. Kit's father began to curse. 'What's up wi' this damned hay?' 'Aye, it's sticking,' said Kit. 'Well, I can't gather it right, it's jammed every way . . . damned stuff's batting at me.' He stood up, half-smothered by an untidy armful, with the expression of a man who is wrestling with an unequal opponent. 'Well, it's got to be done,' said Kit diplomatically. 'I bloody well know it's got to be done! It'll take all night, that's all. It's that bloody new machine of thine.'

Kit had to admit that it was the machine. Somehow it never laid the two layers of a windrow crossed over in the tidy way that an experienced woman raker could do, so that the armfuls you lifted were bound together. But it was cheaper and quicker mowing, and he was not dependent on fickle women to come and help out. Even his father learnt to handle the hay to his reasonable satisfaction after a while, but it certainly was dark before they threw the last of it through the poking-hole into the laithe and trampled it down in the mew.

Slow progress it was, building up a small farm, with many a crisis on the way. Kit had bought a good cow, his only Ayrshire, for most cattle in the Dale were dappled dairy-shorthorns. He paid nineteen pounds and ten shillings for her, and she regularly gave six gallons of milk a day throughout her first winter. Then, when she came to calve, she was stricken with milk fever. So Kit tried the only remedy he knew, took his bicycle pump, connected a tube to it, and pushing it up the teat, began to blow her up in the hope of freeing the blocked milk pipes. Her udders grew distended, fat and bloated under pressure, until they were hard as a football, but no milk would come. So he sealed the teat with grease and left her for a while. When he came back later, milk was beginning to drip from the teats. He milked her well of milk and air, then blew her up again. With a bit of patience she soon recovered. But next year she went down with it again. The old cow doctor said, 'Get rid on her . . . I've never seen one go down three times like that and live.' But Kit kept going with his bicycle pump. Every year the old Ayrshire got milk fever, and every year he blew her up. She survived four inflations before Kit sold her on. What happened to her afterwards, no one knows.

Most farmers in the Dale kept dairy cattle, and they produced a lot of milk. One traditional way of using surplus milk was in the making of Wensleydale cheese. Kit had seen his aunt Nanny making cheese in the farmhouse way and had eaten it many a time as a lad. According to its maturity, the quality of the milk and the length of pressing under a stone cheese-press, its texture and taste could vary considerably. Traditional cheeses were often blue from a beneficent mould, though blue Wensleydale is a rarity today.

The coming of the railways in the late nineteenth century changed the traditional pattern of using surplus milk for cheesemaking because bulk buyers of milk came to the Dale to buy the produce of the larger farms for the growing industrial towns. At about the same time creameries were founded to produce Wensleydale cheese in larger quantities and to a more consistent quality. Hawes creamery began making cheese in 1898 and acquired premises in an old mill beside Duerley beck, a simple stone building above the waterfalls, with its black lettering on the stone-work 'Hawes Creamery'. The carts delivering milk-kits and the pigs squealing in their sties behind the building had been a familiar background to Kit on his way to school.

The small farmers of the Dale, such as Kit, with small quantities of milk, and no cooling systems to prepare the milk for transit on the railway, were dependent on the creamery for the sale of their surplus. They had to scratch hard to make a living, and in hard times many of them would go bust without that little extra. In 1933 times were hard and the steadily worsening agricultural crisis came to a head. Kit was thirty, married, and had been working his farm for seven years, but the prospects were grim. Milk prices were already low, eightpence a gallon in winter and fivepence in summer was all the creamery would pay. Markets were collapsing everywhere. Cheese couldn't be sold for eightpence a pound. Since a gallon of milk makes a pound of cheese, the calculation left no profit for anyone, not even money for overheads or to pay wages.

In the summer of 1933 the ex-army captain who ran the Hawes creamery called all its suppliers together, told them there was no money, not even for milk already supplied, and that he was going bankrupt. The farmers looked at each other in total dismay. With no outlet whatsoever for their milk they too might well be bankrupt within six months. So they talked, and talked, the pubs in Hawes hummed, and at length decided they had no alternative. The creamery must be kept going. They would set up a committee of creditors to run it. Kit, as a respected local man, was appointed to the committee.

Well, they struggled on for a month or two, not very successfully, until in October 1933 the Milk Marketing Board was set up by the government in London in an attempt to deal with the agricultural crisis. The Board would take all good milk from farmers, and pay a normal price for it, which made them secure in the short term, although, of course, the milk must be sold eventually. The question was, how much would the creamery be charged by the Board for milk for cheesemaking. On that price depended the possibility of a profitable operation. If cheese wouldn't sell for more than eightpence a pound, then the committee of creditors, Kit among them, knew they needed a decent margin on the price of a gallon of milk. They hoped that price might be as low as fivepence halfpenny, but were gloomily prepared to pay more. In the meantime they had to operate for two months without knowing the price of their raw materials. At length the Board decided. Hawes creamery would be charged a penny halfpenny per gallon, with a discount of a halfpenny if they collected the milk themselves. A penny a gallon! The committee of creditors drank beer and whisky that night, and, for once, forgot to worry about milk.

Within three months of that magnificent decision the debts had been paid off. The creditors handed the business back to the captain and returned to their farms. Their livelihoods were saved and everything could return to normal. It was like a thunderbolt when, twelve months later, a notice arrived through Kit's door, a circular from the Milk Marketing Board saying that no more milk must be sent to the creamery. The captain was bankrupt again. 'I don't know how he did it,' said Kit to Bob, 'it wasn't bloody possible to go bust!' Kit led a deputation to see the captain, but all he would say was, 'I can't pay . . . They're going to break me . . . I can't pay.' Kit could have shaken the man till he fell apart, which probably wouldn't have taken long. No help there, and yet the creamery must be kept going. All the old arguments still held good. They needed to sell their milk.

The farmers met again, gloom on their faces. Express Dairies had already proposed to buy up all the milk supply in the Dale, and the Board were tempted to accept this easy solution. So were many of the farmers. But without the creamery they would face a monopoly buyer, who was not likely to take small farmers' untreated milk. They would still be driven out. So Kit, wiser from the previous experience and prepared to try anything, took the lead. Some farmers shook their heads. 'Can anyone do better than the captain?' Kit looked at the figures. The price of cheesemaking milk had risen, but only to threepence three-farthings a gallon. 'Well, I can make money out of it,' he said. They all looked at him. Kit was no cheesemaker.

It was a big step for a small tenant farmer, who had risen from farmhand with only an elementary education, to push himself forward at that time of crisis. But Kit was fighting for something that he believed in . . . He was always a farmer at heart, and he knew what would happen to farming in the Dale if this failed. So he began negotiations with the Board, with Express Dairies and with his fellow farmers. It was not so different from cattle-dealing; bargain separately and don't talk too much. Sure enough, Express Dairies wanted the monopoly, and their local agent, a grocer, went the rounds of Hawes and district spreading despair. 'Take no notice of that Kit Calvert . . . he knows nowt about cheese. He'll go t'same way as t'captain, you'll see . . . I can tell you it'll go bust.'

But the Board gave Kit a chance, a little time in which to set up a Company with enough capital to be trusted with the business. It was hard work scraping money out of farmers in the middle of an agricultural depression. Kit himself had to set an example. He managed to put up a hundred pounds, but he had to borrow some of that. Ready money was scarce, and he was taking a big risk. He, too, would be personally bankrupt if the creamery went under again, the farm, stock, and everything gone. The farmers were slow in contributing, though very ready with advice. Kit told the reluctant ones that he couldn't guarantee to take their milk unless they put up at least five pounds. That shamed most of them into putting up ten. Then he had the Company's articles of association drafted with a twenty-five pounds minimum shareholding as a qualification for the Board of Directors. Kit went the rounds again, explaining all this to the uncommercially minded. As he hoped, a fair number said, 'Well, I've putten in ten pounds . . . I'll make it up to twenty-five and perhaps get onto t'board.' And they disappeared upstairs to lift up the mattress. He finally screwed the capital up to the magnificent total of one thousand and eighty-five pounds.

Then Kit really began to mix in top circles. He had to go down to London, to Thames Ditton, for negotiations with officials of the main Board. They insisted on him leaving five hundred pounds deposit with them, for security. Half his painfully garnered capital gone already, or at least, unusable. That left him five hundred and eighty-five pounds for working capital. He had the plant and buildings to buy from the trustee in bankruptcy. The price was eight hundred pounds, good value, but he didn't have it. So then it was a question of re-mortgaging with the bank. High financial negotiations followed and at last his cattle-dealing skills earned him a mortgage of six hundred and fifty pounds. That meant the plant and buildings had cost him a hundred and fifty outright and he had four hundred and thirty-five pounds to start the business.

But Kit was not frightened by this prospect. His secret weapons were the one pound cheese and the pigs. The traditional Wensleydale was made as a big cheese, a millstone in size, for cutting and selling piecemeal in grocer's shops. Those cheeses took at least three weeks to mature on the shelves. The small, round, one pound cheeses took only three days. He could sell his entire month's production of one pound cheeses before the milk cheque for that month was due to the Board. That put his cash flow right at a stroke, though there were many months when he held back the cheque for as long as he dared. He couldn't put off paying too long because of the past history of bankruptcies. At such moments he could only comfort himself with the thought of the five hundred pounds security down at Thames Ditton. But the one pounders were a success, and carried him through.

As for the pigs, one of the side products of cheesemaking was the whey left behind when milk curdled. This was excellent for fattening pigs, and the creamery had a piggery attached, but it was empty, all the pigs sold. So Kit did a deal. He arranged to buy pigs on credit, to be fattened up, with the seller having the option to repurchase them when they were ready for slaughter. That also helped his cash flow, and so he scratted on.

At the first year end the audited profit was one thousand, four hundred and ninety-five pounds. After two years Bob married and Kit handed over the farm to him completely. He had no time for anything but the creamery. He continued to run it, through – and after – the war, as farmers prospered. Finally when he was sixty-five, Kit retired and it was agreed to sell the creamery to the Milk Marketing Board. The price was fixed at half a million pounds, not a bad return for those farmers who put in their grudging twenty-five pounds in 1935.

Once he was comfortably retired Kit built himself a house in Hawes and opened a second-hand bookshop in the market-place, for he had always loved books, and still treasured his first, the *Pronouncing Dictionary* that his father had bought him. He also bought a donkey, and a black and white pony with a trap, to ride through Hawes and the Dales as he had always dreamed he would.

Elsie Wilkinson
in the West Riding

In the days when Yorkshire was divided into three Ridings, the mass of industrial cities, towns and villages that made up the manufacturing strength of the County crowded into part of the West Riding. They were the first offspring of the Industrial Revolution, creatures of coal, steel, engineering, and textiles. Their ranks of stone mills, workshops and houses sprawled up the sides of hills in heady terraces, and a tangle of canals, railways, roads to serve them wound along river valleys. The barren tops of the moors alone remained unconquered, dividing one sooty town from another, retaining a sight, a memory, of the countryside for the 'hands' who laboured the daylight hours away inside the heavy walls of the mills.

Elsie Wilkinson was born in November 1893. Her family moved when she was five to Buttershaw, one of those industrial villages that pocked the landscape south of Bradford. Great Buttershaw Mill took in most of the womenfolk of the village every morning, as they flooded through the gates, past its roman-industrial towers to the weaving shed or spinning floors. Solid Victorian values ruled both labour and life. Elsie grew up knowing that it was best for a girl to work and be quiet, for 'if you listen, you may hear God talking'.

The Silk Dress

Mama made it for her for Whitsuntide, in rich blue lustre, a shiny kind of cotton. It shone like silk. Elsie was extremely proud of that dress. She wouldn't take it off, and Mama warned her about being vain. 'Vanity is a sin, my dear.' They were waiting for Dad to come home after work, and Elsie was looking out of the window for him coming, as she always did. Just to see his tall, athletic figure striding up the street until she could make out his clean-shaven, pale face and dark hair. Dad was always so respectably dressed.

Sometimes Dad would just pick her up and tickle her under the chin before staring intently out of the window. 'We must hurry, sweetheart . . . I want to catch this sky before it changes.' For Dad loved to paint in oils and they often saw amazing, many-coloured sunsets in the evening sky over those rough hills that concealed smoky Halifax.

Mama was speaking. She must attend. 'Your dad'll take you down to buy some boots.' 'Boots,' thought Elsie, 'I don't want boots with this lovely dress.' She had gone home with Doris Kellet, after school, and Doris had taken her up to show the new dress to her mother. 'Mama, look at Elsie's blue silk dress,' and Mrs Kellet had said, 'No, it's not, love. It's not silk.' Elsie was so crestfallen, because she had told everyone at school they must say she was wearing a silk dress and not call it anything but silk. So she told Mrs Kellet, 'No, it is silk!' Mrs Kellet pursed her lips at this inaccuracy, but Doris intervened, saying, 'Elsie likes it to be silk.' 'Oh,' said Mrs Kellet, 'of course it looks like silk, Elsie . . . We'll call it silk because it shines like silk.' Elsie was quite content with that, for, after all, a new dress is important to an eight year old.

'Here comes your Dad,' said Mama, and Elsie looked up from the blue glory around her and saw her beloved father marching up the road. He came in at the door, kissing Mama carefully, for she was expecting a baby, and picked Elsie up. 'Now,' said Mama, 'when you're going down the road don't keep looking down at yourself.' 'Well, I like it,' Elsie replied. 'Yes, but people'll think you've never had a new dress.' Elsie looked glum, so Dad spoke up for her. 'She can look down if she wants, Mother . . . she loves her little dress.' Dad always understood.

So Elsie said, 'All right, Mama,' and she kept her chin up all the way down the road until they were round the corner and out of sight. Then she looked down and the blue was even more glorious in sunset. Dad squeezed her hand, but he said nothing. He was gazing at the sky when she turned to him.

Mama had said, 'Get her some good boots and they'll last her for winter as well.' When they got to the boot shop they looked in the window and Dad said, 'Now then, have you seen any you like?' 'Yes,' said Elsie, drawing in her breath, 'I like those shoes . . . those shoes are lovely, Dad.' They were so dainty, with a strap across the foot and a neat little buckle, much prettier than boots. Dad and Elsie looked at each other from their different heights and the gaslight in the shop window shone on their two pale faces, so similar in colour and proportion that anyone could see the resemblance. Mama sometimes said she had a forehead like alabaster.

'Come along, then,' said Dad, and he led her into the shop and pointed out the shoes in the window. 'What'll Mama say?' 'Oh,' Dad answered, 'I'm buying these.' Elsie remembered to keep her chin up after they turned the corner, though the joy of looking down on a new, blue, silk dress and new shoes was almost too great to bear. She was compelled to skip vigorously every now and then to make up for the stateliness her new grandeur demanded. She thought of Mama once or twice, with a twinge of guilty fear that grew as they approached home.

Mama was waiting in the parlour and she stared. 'Dan, whatever have you bought her shoes for?' 'Oh,' said Dad, carelessly, 'we'll buy her some boots when winter comes.'

Mama was cross. 'You spoil her, you know . . . you spoil her.' Dad laughed at that. 'You can't spoil her,' he said, 'you'll never spoil my Elsie . . . You'll know that some day.'

How Elsie loved her Dad. She loved Mama, of course, but there was a good deal of Christian duty mixed up in that. Dad was like his daughter. He had a sweet nature, and people smiled when they spoke to him. He came of a respectable family and was well educated. In the evenings at home he would play hymns to Mama on his American organ, a beautiful walnut instrument with an inset mirror. Dad could play anything by ear, and his favourite hymn was, 'There were ninety and nine who safely laid in the shelter of the fold.'

Although Dad was the youngest in a family of six, Elsie hardly met her relatives. Buttershaw was a long way from where they lived. She had heard Mama speaking fiercely about Grandfather and Grandmother Askham when it was suggested the children might go for a visit. 'I wasn't good enough for them . . . and my children are too good for them.' Despite her fine, fair hair and blue eyes, Mama could be very fierce at times. She was determined to keep high standards, to have the house spotless and to bring up the children in the fear of God.

God was present always, keeping a regular eye on Elsie's conduct. She knew that if you listened long enough and hard enough you would hear God talking to you. Then you knew what you should do. One Saturday afternoon, Elsie and Doris were going down to the shops. Dad always gave her twopence spending money, which was a lot of money, but he could afford it. They saw an old couple, in rags, shuffling up the road. Elsie noticed their misery and ran over at once to press her twopence into the shaking, grubby hand. 'Bless you, my love,' said the old woman. Elsie knew she was blessed already.

'What are you going to do now,' said Doris, 'you've got no money for sweets.' Elsie smiled. 'I shall get some more, you just see if I don't.' She went round the side of the co-op, faced its sooty wall, put her hands together and closed her eyes. Then she told God what she had done and asked him to give her some more pocket money. Doris just stood and stared.

'Come along,' said Elsie with firm conviction as she led her back up the road and home. Dad was at his easel. She put her arms around his neck and kissed him. Then she told him what she had done. Dad laid down his palette carefully. There was a smell of linseed oil in the air. 'Well done, my sweetheart,' he said, 'here's threepence for you . . . That was a good deed.' Mama came in when she heard the voices. 'What's all this about?' So Dad told her. 'It's a shame,' she said. 'You know they'll only spend it on drink.' Dad smiled. 'If that's what they need, poor things, maybe they do right.' Mama grunted and went back to the kitchen. Elsie reckoned that God was rather like her Dad, only a bit older and not quite so beautiful.

When she was little, before they moved to Buttershaw when Dad became manager of Mr Johnson's Chemical Works, they had lived in a house with a balcony and watched a travelling circus go down the street. She remembered the elephant's long, snaky trunk reaching up to them for food and how she ran inside with fright. She remembered Horace with a tame pigeon that he used to throw under the canal bridge and watch it fly out, poor thing. But Horace was three years older, a big boy who didn't like to play with little sisters. He took her to school but ignored her in the playground.

At Buttershaw school she found a protector in Ralph Wilkinson who was only two years older, ten to her eight. When they teased her because she had such thin legs and called her 'match stalks', Ralph would say 'Leave Elsie alone . . . or I'll box thy ears for thee!' She would smile at him in thanks, and Ralph would blush.

Ralph's father was a barber in Buttershaw and he worked in a wooden shed next to the Furness Inn. Ralph was expected to help out after school hours, and when the clubmen came out of the inn singing 'Sweet Adeline' in chorus it was Ralph's job to sit them down and lather their chins ready for shaving. He had to stand on a buffet to reach. The Wilkinsons weren't in the same class as the Askhams, as Mama told Elsie. So when, after school, Ralph asked her, 'Can I walk thee home, lass?' she answered with a laugh, 'Don't be silly, Ralph . . . I only live across the road.'

Another thing Elsie remembered from before they came to Buttershaw was her last Christmas in the old house. Of course, she had been very little then, but she remembered Mama coming upstairs to ask her if she would like to thank Santa Claus for all the nice things he had brought her. 'Oh, no, Mama,' she said, 'don't let him come upstairs, I'm frightened.' She hid right under the bedclothes at the thought of a stranger in the house. Horace shouted at her from his room not to be a big baby. She heard a heavy tread on the stairs, saw the door open and a robed figure come in, almost falling over its boots. Back under the covers went Elsie, and refused absolutely to come out until Santa Claus was gone. She could hear them all laughing, Mama as well. But she wouldn't come downstairs until he was gone and Dad ran up to fetch her.

Elsie sat in her bedroom sometimes and remembered all these things. She kept out of the way when the new baby was born. Mama had had dead babies once or twice, and it was very sad, she knew. But this one was alive, because she heard it crying. Then her Dad came in to tell her she had a new baby sister who would be called Enid. She wasn't particularly pleased. Later Dad took her to see Mama, who looked tired. When he picked up the baby himself, as gently as though it were a fairy princess, then asked her if she would like to hold her new sister, she at first shook her head. But she saw Dad's concerned smile, and her own good sense came back to her. She looked at her baby sister, and the baby blew a bubble, and Elsie laughed.

A little later in the week, in the evening, Dad was sitting, reading to Mama, when Elsie came in from playing with Doris. 'Dad,' she said excitedly when he had finished a page and kissed her, 'there's such a beautiful doll in the shop. It's lovely, like a princess . . .' and she described its rosebud complexion and lacy clothes. Dad looked at her, and at Mama nursing the new baby. 'Shall we go and see this doll?' he asked. Elsie nodded, wide eyed. Then he got up from his chair, went to the hall, changed out of his slippers and put on his coat. They went down the road, admired the doll together, and Dad took her inside the shop to buy it there and then. What joy! Elsie hardly knew what to say. 'Well,' said Dad, 'it's just something for my Elsie . . . a baby for her.'

They went back home, and Mama, who was still sleepy at times, opened her blue eyes wide when Elsie showed her the doll. She laughed a little when Elsie sat down to nurse her baby, just like Mama. But Elsie heard them afterwards as she sat behind Dad's chair. 'You really do spoil that child, Dan . . . take care or you'll spoil her completely.' 'You know, she won't be spoiled,' Dad answered quietly. 'I don't know that,' Mama retorted. 'Whatever should I do with her if anything happened to you.' 'Now you're being foolish again . . . don't think such things.' Dad went across to comfort Mama and kiss her. Elsie took her doll up to her room.

She soon got accustomed to Enid, who seemed to have come to stay, and she was really quite fond of her sister when she smiled and gurgled. But Dad had been a little serious at times, and she knew there was talk of them moving again as soon as Mama and Enid were ready. Dad would mention it to Mama at times. 'He's done nothing about that leak of gas. I'm sure . . . positive . . . that's what it is. I tell him, "We must get it repaired, Mr Johnson," and he always says, "Yes, I'll get it seen to, Mr Askham." But it's been nearly twelve months now . . . I've got no alternative if he won't listen to me.' 'Did you write for that job in Middlesbrough?' asked Mama. Dad nodded, 'I really think we might have to move. This can't go on.'

It was a Thursday evening, when the ladies came round for their painting class. Dad had been demonstrating oil-painting techniques. He had a landscape on the easel, with one of his dramatic sunsets completed in blood-red and orange. The picture showed a river flowing under a bridge, which was half drawn in. They were having trouble with the perspective view of the bridge, so, at the end of that Thursday evening Dad laid down the brushes and said, 'That's enough. We shall have to finish the bridge next week.'

Still

Dad generally came home for lunch. On Friday he was late. Dinner was spoiling and Mama, getting rather irritated, was feeding the children before sending them back to school. Then they heard a knock at the door. 'Well, that's not Dan,' she said, and went to answer it. A police constable was on the front step. 'Mrs Askham?' he said. 'Yes?' 'Could you come down to the works at once, please, there's been an accident.' Mama stopped in the passage, hand to her chest. She had always had a weak heart. Her white face of fear quelled all their unspoken questions as soon as she appeared in the kitchen. Horace and Elsie stood up without even daring to ask, 'What's the matter, Mama?' It took her almost no time to carry baby Enid next door, to push the two of them off to school, throw a shawl over her shoulders and go flying down Princes Street behind the policeman.

When Elsie and Horace got to school some of the lads knew all about it. 'Thy Dad's hurt bad,' they said, 'bleedin' on his head . . . and Harry's dead.' Elsie knew it was true, because they weren't teasing. She couldn't possibly go into school, even though nothing could really hurt her Dad. She had to know the worst and he might need her. Didn't he often call her his 'little oak tree'? So she left the playground and followed Mama down to the works. It wasn't like her. She was normally an obedient child, but this was for her Dad.

When she saw the grimy, dismal face of the works and

its staring windows she hardly dared go closer. It all looked so cruel. But something was happening at the door. A horse ambulance had drawn up outside and there was Mama, climbing in. They must have Dad inside already. He'd be going to hospital. She should be with him. Elsie began to run forward, the tears in her eyes. But the horses broke into a trot and the ambulance began to pull away from her. She hadn't the wind to shout 'Stop! stop! Wait for me!' So she stumbled to a halt, to stand in the roadway looking down at her match-stalk legs, the fine shoes on her feet and the dirty granite setts of the roadway, all blurring in her sight as she panted for breath. Elsie turned away from her father's path at last, and wandered emptily towards home. After a while she began to worry about school. Would she get the cane for running away?

Neighbours took her in, and no awkward questions were asked. They waited and Enid had to be nursed, which was a comfort. The waiting seemed to go on forever. Mama didn't return home until the evening. They could see from her face that things were bad. Her look was heavy, drawn and angry. When they were in the parlour Mama pushed them into chairs. She was silent for a moment or two, playing with the fringe of her shawl. This was not like her. Then she spoke. 'Your dad's dead,' she said, 'dead . . . He was still alive when we got to the Infirmary . . . but he died at five o'clock . . . just after the clock struck.'

Elsie began to cry, but it was really because she knew she should, and because Mama was so tight in her grief. The real knowledge of Dad's leaving would come later and in odd ways, at little moments when he should be there. But she could see the painting on the easel, with its glorious sunset and the unfinished bridge. Somehow that was more sad than anything else, more real. The bridge would never be painted now. That was what it meant. Elsie went over to Mama and put her arms round the shawl. She was a loving little girl. Mama's hair smelt sooty.

'When my little Emma died,' said Mama, 'she had such blue eyes, and lovely golden curls . . . She was so good.' Mama was looking right through the parlour wall, as if she wasn't really with them at all. 'She used to come home from school with a sweet in her hand, and she'd say . . . "I've saved this for you, Mama . . . Betty gave it me and I thought you'd like it." She was so good . . . I remember . . . she used to say, "I've washed up, Daddy, and tidied up, can I read my book . . ." ' Mama didn't speak for a while, but she was still staring through the parlour wall. Elsie kept as quiet as she could, hardly breathing. Horace didn't fidget. Mama was almost whispering to herself when she spoke again. 'When she got it, the scarlet fever . . . she was just five and a half, so pretty . . . I said to God when she died, and I couldn't help it, I said to God "If you wanted one of my children why didn't you take that one? Take Elsie, I've only had her six months." '

Elsie was still for about a minute, then she began to cry into Mama's lap, which also smelt sooty, but that was Bradford. 'Hush, child,' said Mama in a comforting fashion. One word of kindness was all that Elsie needed, and she began to sob in earnest. 'Didn't you want me . . . didn't you want me, Mama?' Mama seemed not to know what she was talking about, as if she hadn't realized she had been speaking. 'Of course I wanted you,' she said, 'of course.'

Mama blamed Mr Johnson for Dad's death, saying how Dad had asked him time and again to mend the gas leak by the still. Eventually she was told the full story when Arthur Warbrick came up from the works to pay his respects. They had been cleaning out the still, which was a huge metal cylinder, nine feet high, with an iron spike in the centre. A ladder went up the outside and another down the inside. Because Dad was worried about the escape of gas he always stood beside the still when it was being cleaned and had the man inside come up every five minutes to report.

That Friday he looked at his watch. 'Time's gone.' There was no sign of Harry. 'He should be up by now' . . . Dad began to climb the ladder. 'Don't go in, Dan,' they said, 'don't go, it'll kill thee.' Dad shook his head at them. 'Get out of the way,' and he went on. At the top he looked back. 'One of you come up this ladder and help me out,' he added, climbed over the lip and vanished inside. The men who waited could hear him dragging the heavy body of the unconscious man, hear his burdened, laborious steps up the ladder. He reached the top, stretched out a hand to be helped out, missed his grip and fell back the full height, his head striking the metal spike. When they got him out, Harry was dead.

Arthur Warbrick told them something else, which never came out at the inquest, or later. After the accident Mr Johnson had got all the men together. 'Now,' he said, 'I don't want to hear one word about any escape of gas . . . don't you talk to anyone about what happened. If you do . . . I'll sack the lot of you.'

The inquest was delayed for a while for the accident to be investigated, but in the end no blame was laid on anyone and the verdict was accidental death. Mama was to get only the standard compensation. Poor Arthur Warbrick didn't dare look her in the face afterwards. 'I ought to have spoken,' he kept saying. 'Poor Mrs Askham . . . three little-uns to bring up in a world like this.'

The compensation was slow in coming, and Elsie remembers being dragged past the dreadful chemical works to Mr Johnson's grey house on the hill. Mama marched across the garden to rap on the door. She had swallowed her pride enough to ask for the money that was due to her, but she didn't like it. A servant brought Mr Johnson to the door. 'It hasn't come yet, Mrs Askham,' he said, 'but I'll give you an advance.' Then he added, shrewdly, 'I know I'll get it back.' This was just too much for Mama. She shoved Elsie forward into full view. 'Yes, but my lass won't get her father back.' Mr Johnson made no reply.

Living with Mother

Mother found another house for them, a cottage down Manorley Lane. It was further out of Buttershaw, and a longer walk to get anywhere. They only had two bedrooms, which meant a curtain across one corner for Horace, but at least the rent was much lower than their old house. Mother turned a determined face to the world and made sure she kept up their standards. Whatever happened, the Askhams were going to be decently dressed, have a good, clean house and behave as respectable people should.

It cost Mother a lot of effort to keep to such standards. All the happy extravagances of Dad's days were gone. Life became bitter with the grinding labour of the poor. Mother took in washing at twopence halfpenny a pound and was up till midnight, night after night, ironing it. She went out cleaning offices and scrubbing floors. She would ask no charity from Dad's family, though at times her weak heart fluttered madly as if in protest at the effort of it. At such times she would remain erect, face white as a corpse, and clasp her hands to her side, but her look remained one of iron determination. The body must do what the will demanded.

Several people tried to help, particularly Mrs Nicholls, the schoolmaster's wife, who lived further down Manorley Lane. One Sunday afternoon they were at home, and Elsie was nursing baby Enid, when they heard voices outside and a knock at the door. Mother went to open it, and a very respectable-looking couple, a grey-haired man and his wife, asked if they could come in, explaining that they were friends of the Nicholls. They seemed to have a rather embarrassed manner, but Mother got them a cup of tea and they tactfully mentioned Dad's accident. Then the lady began to explain that their own children were grown up, that they missed family life, and were thinking of adopting a child. Would it not be a help to Mother to relieve her of one of her burdens and guarantee the child a good home. Elsie was shaken. She listened in amazement to this preposterous idea and clutched hard at baby Enid just in case they should snatch her and make off with their prize. Tears came to her eyes. It might be Elsie herself who would have to go. After what Mother had said about baby Emma's death, after Dad's death, could she rely on home at all?

Mother sat upright in her chair, pale as if she was having an attack. Then she caught fire. 'Only God can take my children from me,' she said. 'As for giving them away . . . you might as well take a knife and cut out my heart. I shall never part with them!' She glared at the poor, kindly lady as if she were a representative of the whole cruel world and all its miseries. The lady burst into tears and half-audible apologies. Elsie began to cry as well. She laid Enid on Mother's lap and threw her arms protectively round the pair of them. That was how the elderly couple left the Askhams, creeping shamefacedly away from such a demonstration of domestic loyalty, though they had meant nothing but good. The family would stay together, whatever happened. Elsie was so willing, so determined, after that, to do her part in support of her brave mother.

She could do very little, a thin girl of nine, except help at home and look after the baby. One evening Mother was ironing and she looked at Elsie as the child came down from putting Enid to bed. 'Go on, lass,' she said, 'you've been nursing baby ever since school. Now get out, and get some fresh air.' So Elsie took her skipping rope and went outside. But she only skipped half-heartedly, once or twice, forwards and backwards, no singing or counting. Then she stopped, and thought, 'I don't know how we're going to manage.' The rope hung limply from her hand. 'I wonder how I can earn some money?' She looked down the lane to Mrs Nicholls' house. Then she screwed up her courage and went and knocked at the door.

Mrs Nicholls opened it, and looked at the thin-legged, serious little girl on the threshold. 'Hello, Elsie.' 'Mrs

Nicholls,' she said, all in a gabble. 'Mrs Nicholls, I just wondered, perhaps, if you needed any help in the house?' 'Oh,' said Mrs Nicholls, and hesitated, then she smiled, 'Come in, Elsie . . . Yes . . . Yes I do need some help. What can you do?' 'Well,' Elsie answered, businesslike at once, 'I can wash-up, and I don't break any cups or plates . . . and I can clean the knives and forks and spoons . . . and dust the parlour. I can go on all your errands all week long . . . and I never make mistakes with money.'

'Well,' said Mrs Nicholls, and there was a tear in the corner of her eye, 'you're just the person I'm wanting. When can you start?' 'Oh,' said Elsie, 'right now . . . Mother thinks I'm playing out.' 'You're a right good girl, will you start now? Come along.' Mrs Nicholls took her down to the cellar. It was lovely, clean and airy, white-washed, and on the shelf stood a round, wooden machine for cleaning knives. So Elsie cleaned the knives. After that she washed up.

Then it was time to dust the parlour. Mrs Nicholls gave her two dusters. 'Won't one be sufficient, Mrs Nicholls?' 'No, dear, you hold the furniture with one duster and polish it with the other. Then you don't leave finger marks.' 'Oh,' said Elsie, 'I never thought of that.' She finished her jobs, and Mrs Nicholls gave her some pennies. She took them straight back to Mother and, though Mother frowned a little at first at the thought of her daughter working for Mrs Nicholls, and Elsie trembled in case she was rejected, in the end Mother was pleased and gave her a kiss, after she had accepted the money.

They did need money. Horace wasn't a great deal of help even though he had started work as a grocer's boy. His wages were very low and he didn't do much at home, but, after all, he was a man. Those three years after Dad's death aged Mother, cutting lines round her mouth and eyes, etching the outward form of her bitter determination.

They must earn more money to live decently. So, as soon as Elsie was twelve, she went to work half-time. Dad had hoped to keep her on at school, but that was over. The first week she began at six in the morning, and finished at twelve-thirty. In the afternoon she went to school. As a half-timer she only got paid four shillings and sixpence a week, but even that was a help. Mother had got her started on the spinning floor at Bottomley Brothers Mill in Buttershaw. Young girls were wanted there because they had supple fingers for mending breaks in the thread as it was spun out at high speed. So Elsie began work among the roaring, black machines, in the smell of oil, piecing together fine yarns in early morning gaslight. One hundred stone steps up to the spinning floor on her thin legs to start work at six. She was determined to be always on time and a good worker. They needed the money.

As soon as she was thirteen Elsie could begin to work full-time, a fifty-four-hour week for nine shillings pay. Things were less desperate for Mother after that, she had less need to drive herself to take on work and could spend more time looking after the house. She had two children working now and only Enid dependent. But that didn't mean she could relax her eternal vigilance.

Elsie always came home for dinner, and one day Mother asked her to bring back a quarter of tomatoes for old Mrs North, who lived round the corner. Mother had brought the children up to help the unfortunate whenever they could, for that was part of the proper standard. So Elsie said, 'Of course I will,' and called at the greenhouses near Buttershaw Mill. Two biggish tomatoes came to just about a quarter pound, so she took them and walked on home, a little tired after her ten hours in the close atmosphere of the spinning room. She was still a spindly child at thirteen.

Mother took the tomatoes round to Mrs North while Elsie was setting out the tea things, but she came back with them. 'Oh, Elsie,' she said, 'will you take these back. It won't take you long. Just tell him she wants smaller ones, she doesn't want two big ones.' Elsie suddenly felt angry. She was tired. She wanted her tea. She didn't want to walk all the way down to the mill and back again. 'No, I won't,' she said, astounded at her own defiance. Mother stared at her in astonishment. A rebellion in the family.

'You mean you're really saying no . . . to me!' Elsie was quiet for a moment, she was close to tears, but this was too much. 'Yes, I do,' she said. 'If you'd asked me to do it for yourself I'd have gone right away . . . but then, of course, you wouldn't ask me a thing like that for yourself. I'm not going for Mrs North!' Mother held her clenched hands to her sides. 'You won't?' 'No, I will not do it.'

Mother took the tomatoes back to Mrs North. When she came in she wouldn't speak to Elsie. If there was one thing Mother would never accept, it was disobedience. After tea they had a bowlful of apples as pudding. Elsie loved apples, and Mother knew it. 'Horace, Enid, would you like an apple?' she said. She didn't offer one to Elsie at all and Elsie knew better than to ask. So Elsie sat there nursing her indignation. Enid was only six years old, but she sympathized. 'Have some of mine,' she whispered to her elder sister, and Elsie replied, 'It would choke me!'

She found a new friend in Buttershaw as she grew older and a little bigger. Nellie was a lively, outgoing girl who made her laugh. Nellie was always full of fun. She had green eyes and golden hair and wore Dolly Varden hats. Mother didn't like her and wasn't sparing in her judgement. 'I don't like Nellie. I don't like you going out with her. I don't trust her.' She saw Nellie as representative of all she distrusted and feared in the Twentieth Century. Elsie would answer, calmly, 'Well, you trust me and then you'll not have anything to fear.' And Mother would eye her simply-dressed daughter, so young for her age, not like that minx Nellie, with a stern complacency. 'Ah . . . I know I'll get the truth out of you!'

But like and unlike may call to each other, and Elsie had a dear friend in Nellie, getting sympathy and encouragement when Mother bore down too heavily. Nellie had a good job in an office in Halifax, and she lived a thoroughly modern life. 'Why don't you learn,' she asked Elsie, and lent her a Pitman's Shorthand book. Elsie was keen and worked herself in the evenings until she could take a hundred words a minute. They used to write to each other in shorthand, which infuriated Mother because, though she always opened the notes, she couldn't read what they said. This also didn't endear Nellie to her.

When Elsie was fifteen, Nellie said, 'Elsie, I think there's a job coming in our office. Do you fancy working with me?' 'Oh, Nellie,' said Elsie, and nodded her enthusiasm, for Nellie knew how keen she was to work with pen in hand at a quiet desk. So Nellie took some soundings in Halifax, and it all seemed possible. Elsie could almost certainly have the job and she would be better paid and have more time at home. How marvellous, like a dream come true, like a breach in the spinning-shed wall to let Elsie out to find a daylit future. Elsie went to bed with her head full of smart ambitions, nice hats to wear to work, clean blouses, a quiet desk and perhaps young men to smile at. On Sunday morning, before church, she told the good news to Mother.

So pleased and proud to have found a better fortune for the family, something more respectable and better paid, even though she was only fifteen, Elsie chattered on. Her pale face hovered excitedly over the breakfast cups. She hardly noticed that Mother was silent, for Mother could be very silent at times.

'Have you finished?' She suddenly took in Mother's grim expression. 'Yes, Mother.' 'Well, you can't go . . .' Elsie opened her mouth to protest, but was allowed no time. 'Oh no, you can't go . . . you're going to be a weaver.' 'But . . . Mother . . .' 'There's too much temptation in an office!' 'But, Mother, I'll have a lot more money for us all . . . and I needn't start so early. It's eight o'clock instead of six . . . don't you think?' Mother rose in majestic, black, implacability from the breadcrumbs, as solid as Bottomley Brothers Mill, and as immovable. 'Now we won't argue. There's no need to speak of it again. There's nothing to speak about . . . You're going to be a weaver . . . now get that into your mind.'

When Elsie told Nellie what had happened she was too amazed even to laugh. 'I don't know how you stick it, I really don't.' When Elsie gave the details of what Mother had said, she just whistled as loudly as she could, which was pretty loud, and said, 'That was Queen Victoria.' Elsie had to admit she was right, though she had not the slightest intention of disobeying Mother. She simply couldn't face that stony silence for weeks and months.

Fortunately, Mother didn't try to stop her seeing Nellie, which she could well have done. Elsie was very fond of Nellie, and might have had a real row with Mother over a friend – something she would never contemplate if only her own little dreams were at stake. But Mother knew, sometimes, when to temper the wind. So, on a sunny evening when Nellie called for Elsie, and said, 'Shall we go boating in Wibsey Park?' and Elsie asked, 'Is it all right, Mother?' Mother answered quickly and cheerfully, 'Go on, love, it'll do you good.' Since Elsie didn't get any pocket-money she gave her twopence. It was twopence for half an hour on the boats. Elsie put the money in her little leather purse and went upstairs to get ready. Nellie followed.

Well, Nellie was giggling away, full of fun, quite impossible to hush, and Elsie could imagine Mother listening icily downstairs. 'Come here,' said Nellie, in a commanding whisper as she shoved Elsie down on the bed and opened her handbag, spreading powder, rouge, lipstick and face-cream on the cover. Elsie stared. 'No . . . I can't have that!' Mother wouldn't even let her use face-cream. Nellie put her finger to Elsie's lips and sat down beside her to giggle for a moment. Then, when her hands were steadier, she started on the beautification of Elsie.

'Mother won't let me have it!' 'Hush, you look beautiful!' 'Well, she won't let me go.' Nellie was spreading the lipstick with a careful finger. 'Hold your lips still . . . when you get down the stairs, just turn your face away. That's all you need to do.' So they finished this top-secret operation, and Elsie put her coat on, and Nellie tried to stop giggling. They marched solemnly down stairs. Elsie kept her face turned away. 'We're going now, Mother.' 'When you've washed your face, my dear.' That was that. Mother always knew. Elsie went into the kitchen and washed herself at the sink. When they went out again, Mother said nothing.

But Nellie was impossible. As soon as they were at Black Hill, and out of sight, she stopped Elsie. 'I'm going to put you some more on.' 'Don't be silly, Nellie.' 'No, you're going to be beautiful today, it's important.' 'Why, Nellie, when we're only going boating?' Nellie cascaded into giggles. 'How'll we get it off?' 'Oh you just spit on your hanky.' 'I don't know what you're making all this fuss for, Nellie.' But Elsie was duly beautified, if puzzled.

'Come along,' said Nellie, 'we're going to be late.' 'How do you mean, late? We're in our own time, aren't we?' But at the park gates there were two young men waiting, Johnny and Tom from the church choir. They raised their trilbys and spoke in chorus, 'Good evening, girls.' Elsie gave Nellie one long look of reproachful admiration. Nellie had to stop and giggle again in reply. 'Come on,' said Johnny, 'we've got the boats. There's nothing to wait for. We've got the boats all ready.'

'Well,' Elsie said, 'here's the money, Johnny.' Johnny shook his head. 'Now don't insult me, Elsie. It's the man's job to pay.' Now Elsie was really quite fond of him, but she held out the money, all the same. 'If you don't take that twopence I won't go in the boat . . . my Mother wouldn't let me go if she knew you were paying for me.' 'But your Mother likes our family.' 'Yes, I know she does, but I've still got to pay.' So she pressed the twopence on him, and he returned it, and in the end it went in the water, purse and all.

At least Elsie wouldn't still have that hot, guilty money heavy in her hand, but she regretted the loss of her leather purse. Johnny rowed her round the lake and she wondered if she could possibly look as pretty as Nellie did when the evening sunshine lit her golden hair. Johnny was good, and kind and respectful. When they reached the park gate he asked her to meet him again. 'No,' she said, 'I can't meet you. Mother doesn't know I've come out with you.' 'Go on, Elsie, you can meet me, it can't do any harm.' 'No, I can't. I can't ask Mother . . . and besides, I can't go out with boys . . . I really can't . . . she needs me.'

Nobody likes bad warps

'She's going too far, you know.' Nellie's beautiful green eyes looked positively malicious as she said it. 'Not at all,' said Elsie gently, 'not at all. She is my Mother, you know . . . Remember that.' Nellie frowned, then put an arm round her friend's waist and sighed sympathetically. 'You're unique, you know.' Elsie sensed the continued criticism behind the flattery. 'It's true,' she protested, 'that's the way I want it . . . she's my Mother . . . and everybody respects her.'

Elsie made a good weaver, for she also did her best and Mother had told her regularly since she was a little girl: 'If a thing's worth doing at all, it's worth doing well.' Though her heart was still in doing office-work, clean, interesting and busily quiet as she saw it, with piles of white paper on the desks, still she didn't grudge her work at the mill. She gave them a good ten hours' worth and then went home to the housework.

Elsie was rather tired one Friday evening when she walked along Manorley Lane from the mill. It was drizzling and she huddled in her thick coat. Mother always saw that they dressed well and Elsie was learning to make more of the family clothes. It would be good to sit down for a moment in the warm and have a cup of tea. She lifted the latch of the door. Mother got up from her chair as soon as it was open a crack. Mother was breathing hard. What could be the matter? She had an envelope in her hand. 'What's this, then?' she asked angrily. 'Hello, Mother.' 'What's this? I said . . . How long has this been going on?' 'What is it, Mother?' 'Read it! Read it!' and she thrust the envelope into Elsie's hand.

It was a love letter. It began 'Dearest Elsie', and went on beautifully as she read it, slowly, with trembling, cold hands. She really began to feel how sad it was, and how nice, and when she came to the signature she understood. It was John, the baritone soloist in the church choir. He was twenty-one, she knew, and had tried to speak to her once or twice at choir practice, though she had thought nothing of it. It seemed that all that year when she was seventeen he had been admiring her over the top of his music book. How lovely.

But Mother was breathing at her elbow. 'Did you know about this?' 'No, Mother.' 'I see.' She breathed out again, an audible hissing. 'Take that pen . . . there's paper here.' 'What shall I say?' 'I'll tell you.' Mother dictated a stern refusal, watching over Elsie's shoulder to see that she got it all down. John must never speak or write to Elsie again. Elsie thought it was so unfair to the poor man, he had meant very well, but he simply didn't understand. So, when Mother left her alone to seal up the envelope she scribbled a quick note in explanation and promised to meet him to set things right. How her heart beat as she did it. What would Mother say if she found out? It didn't bear thinking about.

Nellie arranged for Elsie to come to tea on Saturday, and John was there, of course, for Nellie hadn't yet given up hope of converting her friend to modern ways. Elsie was quite frank and open to him. She was very, very sorry, but it couldn't be done, she had her duties, and they came first. So poor John went despondently away and Elsie walked home rather sadly, but firm in her duty. John wouldn't give up. He waited for her outside the mill. Whenever Nellie proposed a little trip, a walk or a visit, it was always with John in mind. Nellie thought this was the best way to give Elsie 'a real life' as she called it.

In the end Elsie had to give Nellie up for a while and stick at home. After that she saw very little of John, though to think of him made Elsie pleasantly sad. One evening, months later, Mother had taken Enid out and Elsie was alone, when the farmer's wife popped her head in the kitchen door. 'There's a young man here wants to see thee.' 'Well, I'm sorry, but I really can't . . .' She knew it must be John. 'He says, "Is there no hope?"' 'No, I can't.'

e school

iriam today

Approach to Bradford

Jack at the wheel

Jack today

ad to the quarry

rtersett now

The old creamery

Kit today

The chemical works

Spinning (Bradford Industrial Museum)

sie today   Buttershaw Mill

Planting the penny-hedge (Doran Bros., Whitby)

Old Whitby (Doran Bros., Whitby)

Lawrie today

wrie standing before the mainsail of the Whitby lifeboat

ook Street

Bert today

The pipe maker (J. D. Simson, Beverley)

Jennie tod

On the keel

'Well, he says he's off to Australia.' 'I just can't . . . I can't speak to him.' The head vanished and John went to Australia. Elsie sat over the boot last, repairing the family shoes, and hammered her thumbs instead of the leather whilst she thought about it all.

Poor lads, she loved them all, they were a grand lot. Ralph Wilkinson now, who had saved her from torment at school ten years ago and whose father was barber in Buttershaw, he was one other. Ralph had proposed to her as soon as she was seventeen, and he kept on doing it every month. He said he'd go on until she gave in. But Elsie could laugh at Ralph's goings on, in the kindest possible way, of course. It didn't have the desperate sadness of John's despair. The older boys seemed to be more serious, and she had to be very tactful so as not to hurt their feelings. 'I love you all,' she said, 'you're lovely.' 'Well, if we are, why don't you let us take you out?' 'Well, I can't . . . I've got to keep the home going.'

Irvine was an overlooker at Buttershaw Mill and came from a respected local family. He was twenty-five and earning a good wage. One afternoon he stopped Elsie in the mill and said, 'Would you like to come to the Messiah on Saturday, in St George's Hall?' 'Oh,' she answered, 'I'd love to . . . but Mother would never allow it. I can tell you that right away.' Irvine nodded gravely. He had known Mother since he was six, when the Askhams came to Buttershaw. 'I'll come round tonight and ask her, Elsie,' he said.

Elsie feared the consequences if Mother was asked outright, so she tried to prepare the ground. Of course, Mother was on to it like a shot. 'What's all this about?' So Elsie told her. She sucked in her cheeks. 'Well, it can do no harm, I suppose,' she said. Elsie was radiant, but amazed. She really wanted to go. 'Provided,' Mother added remorselessly, 'his sister goes as well. You must be chaperoned, my love.'

So, when Irvine arrived, Mother was most affable, sat him down, offered him tea and asked after his family. When it came to the Messiah, Irvine explained that he only had two tickets. His sister was not going. 'Oh,' said Mother, 'then Elsie can't go, Irvine.' 'But why, Mrs Askham, you know I'll take care of her?' 'I thought as much,' said Mother. 'There can be no question of that. I'm afraid I cannot allow you to take Elsie out at all!' 'But . . . Mrs Askham!' Irvine was dumbfounded. 'You may invite her again when she is twenty-one, but till then I will not permit you to see Elsie. It is my responsibility.' She took no heed of Irvine's protests.

Irvine was a hard-working and persistent man, schooled by his background not to give in easily. He asked Elsie to elope with him. He had everything planned, and his sister's support in looking after Elsie until they could marry. 'Your Mother'll have a better chance, you know, Elsie. She's daft not to see it. With both of us earning she'd never need to work again.' Elsie told him that she knew Mother best, and Mother wouldn't accept charity from anyone. There was no question of any elopement.

Then Mother intercepted one of Irvine's letters. Elsie had never seen her so furious, white-faced and rigid on the hearthrug, her clenched fists reflected in the blackleading. 'I shall go to a solicitor,' she said. 'No, Mother, don't.' 'You be quiet, Elsie . . . To think of luring my daughter from me . . . and then offering charity to me!' She did go to a solicitor and paid him to send Irvine a letter warning him not to molest Elsie in any way. She also made Elsie leave her job at the mill, where she would have to see Irvine every day. Elsie had to take another job at a mill a mile further away, which meant another twenty minutes walk each way, morning and evening, rain or frost. It took about a year of this misery before Irvine was convinced of his folly and she could return to Buttershaw Mill.

To give Mother her due, once Enid was old enough to leave school and start work, as Elsie had done, Mother herself took work as a weaver. It was hard for her at first, though Elsie taught her and helped out. Mother was at her elbow all the time in the weaving shed, though, mercifully, she couldn't say much above the racket of the looms. But Elsie never got away from supervision at all. Mother wasn't well. Her heart condition, after those nine births and the years of scraping, always troubled her, made her breathless and sometimes irritable.

Elsie herself was one of the best weavers in the mill by the time she was eighteen. They employed her to produce the patterns of cloth that would go out as samples all over the world. She worked on broad looms where the shuttle had a long travel across the shed of the loom and so the machine must be set up absolutely right to maintain an even weave. Sometimes she did special work, on jacquard looms, where the warp was controlled by punched cards folding down like a pianola roll. It made lovely, detailed designs, birds and flowers. 'Elsie can weave any mortal thing,' they said, and they paid her extra to teach newcomers. But still she not only did her own work, but looked after Mother as well, carrying her completed pieces of cloth upstairs for finishing, collecting new bobbins for her when the weft was running out.

Mother was given looms at the end of the big shed among some of the old ladies who had been sixty years in weaving but were now slowing down. They were the poorer end of trade, working more slowly and so earning less. Yet they always seemed to get the bad warps, when their looms were set up for a new piece of cloth and the giant rolls of yarn were fitted to run through the working parts of the machine to where the shuttle was beaten to and fro carrying the weft. Bad yarn, it was, that broke all across the shed of the loom when the weave tightened, so that the loom must be stopped and the broken end pieced in, so losing time and money. All day the loose ends would drop down, and Mother would grit her teeth to bend into the loom and sort it out.

'Oh, I am tired,' she said one day at dinner. 'You know, they've put me another bad warp in.' Elsie knew it wasn't fair. 'Good,' she said. 'That's the last you'll get!' As soon as the wheels began to turn again she went across to the warping shed. 'Where's the manager?' 'Hello, Elsie . . . what do you want?' Elsie looked daggers at him as a monster of oppression. 'Now then . . . if you bring any more bad warps to either my Mother or those old ladies, I'll ask for my cards!' 'You can't do that, Elsie.' 'I'm telling you now . . . If you've any good warps, then put 'em on the old folks' looms – we young-uns can stand it.'

She went back to the weaving shed. Within five minutes, Mr White, the weaving manager, was standing beside her. 'You're not going to leave us, Elsie?' he mouthed over the rumble of the looms. 'If there's any bad warps I shall go, certainly!' It was not often Elsie spoke her mind so determinedly, but this time it seemed to work. They had much better warps.

A week or so later Elsie was going to dinner when she came on a lass of about her own age, crying. 'What's the matter, Annie?' she asked. 'I've got a right bad warp.' 'Well, you've never had one before, have you?' 'No . . . I don't like it at all.' Elsie offered her no sympathy, just the consolations of homespun philosophy. 'Nobody likes bad warps . . . but you get 'em all the same.'

Little Emma

Ten years of weaving, ten years of looking after the house and being the breadwinner, and Elsie was twenty-five. The First World War was drawing to its bloody close. Mother decided that, in the new, post-war world, Elsie could be allowed some pocket-money. She gave her one shilling and sixpence a week and regularly asked her what she had done with it. 'Well, I haven't spent it yet, Mother. I'm saving up for some perfume.' 'Oh, I'll buy you some perfume,' said Mother, for she did like to see her daughter happy, when it was practical. So she bought Elsie a tiny bottle and Elsie was duly grateful.

Time passed and Horace, being a man and therefore free to do such things, married and left home. Mother spoke to the farmer next door and arranged to rent one of his cottages. It was cheaper, only half a crown a week, and quite convenient, though they had to put up with only one bedroom, a large attic room with box stairs rising straight from the kitchen. They had two big beds, one for Mother, the other for Elsie and Enid.

It was becoming more and more of a problem to get Mother out of bed and down to Buttershaw Mill for six o'clock start-up each morning. Not through lack of determination, that was never Mother's problem, but simply that her heart couldn't move her body well enough. Even when she was getting dressed Mother had to pause, sit on the bed, and pant for breath. Walking her down to the mill on a hot August day, when there was no freshness in the air, left even Elsie tired.

On one such morning the manager watched Elsie helping her Mother into the weaving shed. He seemed thoughtful as he retired into the office. At dinner-time he stopped her outside the shed. 'Elsie.' 'Yes, Mr White.' 'You're the highest paid weaver we've got . . . and a damned good one too.' He paused. 'Well, what are you getting at?' 'I think it's a shame you're paying all that income tax . . . I can see your Mother's getting tired, and . . . I'm not sure we can keep her on much longer . . .' Now Elsie really knew this was true. She was already fetching and carrying everything for both sets of looms and now, more and more, she had to tend Mother's looms for her as well. So she nodded, thoughtfully, and Mr White went on, encouraged. 'Don't you think it'd be a good thing if she stayed at home? There'd be less tax to pay, so you wouldn't be much worse off . . . You get her to stay at home.'

Elsie really expected ructions about this. The thought of even implying weakness directly to Mother frightened her. But, oddly enough, Mother took it like a lamb. She obviously felt more tired than she showed. Like a rusty clock, all her movements became slow and painful once she stopped regular work. She kept the house clean for a while, but soon they had to get a wheelchair for her and it was an effort to help her up to bed. But she was the same gritty Mother in spirit, even so. Enid dreamed of becoming a nurse, just as Elsie longed for an office, and the answer was the same. 'Get down to the mill!' Mother believed in keeping the family together.

One morning at work Elsie put the looms on and went down for a board full of fresh bobbins. She was teaching young Kenneth at the time, one of the manager's sons. He was a nice lad of seventeen, and she rather liked him. It made her a little thoughtful when he told her, confidentially, about his romantic, imaginary, love life with the distant typist in the mill office. She made a good listener and was very quiet, for she liked Kenneth and was rather prone to dream herself. So, when Norman stopped her on her way back to the shed, she hardly listened to what he was saying.

'Just a minute, Elsie. Just a minute . . . I want to have a word with thee.' 'I can't, me loom's going.' 'Just a minute.' Norman took part of the weight of her board and the heap of bobbins on it rocked unsteadily. He looked at her, red-faced above the bobbins. Only that morning his mother had been telling her what a good lad he was. 'Will you marry me, Elsie . . .', he was off on a gallop through his laboriously prepared speech, which gave Elsie time to steady her thoughts and the bobbins. 'I'm twenty-one today . . . I've done me time now. I'm a fully-fledged overlooker, Elsie . . . one day I'll be a manager. Will you marry me?'

What with the bobbins, the waiting looms, which might be doing anything by now, and the feeling of deadening duty in her own heart, Elsie hadn't her normal tact. 'No . . . you must be joking!' 'I'm not joking. I wouldn't joke about a think like that . . . you ask my mother. She wants it too, you know. I'm twenty-one today.' Elsie looked at his honest, hopeful face and felt ready to cry. 'Yes, and I'm thirty-one.' 'You're younger than lasses of twenty-one.' 'Maybe you think so, but I am thirty-one.'

She turned and hurried off, leaving Norman in no doubt that his case was hopeless. But Elsie was beginning to think her future was hopeless, too. All those lovely boys had spoken to her of love through the years. Duty had said 'no'. Now she had been a working woman for nearly twenty years. There was young Kenneth, seventeen, working beside her, and she could have loved him, but he confided in her as if she were a grandmother. She was thirty-one, and her life seemed set for ever in its old pattern.

When Elsie came home that evening Mother had got some stew cooked and they ate in silence. Then Mother asked to be taken out for some air, so Elsie wheeled her down Manorley Lane. It was a hard struggle getting back, uphill, for Mother had got heavier since she stopped working and Elsie only weighed eight stone. When they were back inside, Elsie sat down for a moment. Mother had unwrapped her shawl, laid it down and looked at her. 'It's the night for blackleading, Elsie,' she said. Time to start on the housework, tired as she was. She glared at the kitchen range, sitting there, waiting to be polished, making demands on her as if it were a . . . relative.

After a while Mother became so ill that she had to stay in bed. They called in Dr Robinson from Low Moor and, after a couple of visits, he took Elsie aside. 'I'm sorry about your Mother, Miss Askham . . . but I really can't do anything more for her.' Mother knew what it meant. She had been bedridden for two years and didn't expect to get up again. Elsie was getting very tired with work, keeping the house, and looking after an invalid. Mother caught hold of her hand. Her face was flushed, she might almost have been crying. 'It makes me sad, love, to think of leaving my children alone in this world.'

Elsie used to lie in bed beside Enid when she was too weary to sleep right away, and hear Mother's restless breathing, the fidgeting with her bedclothes and the fighting for breath. The bedroom had smelt of sickness for years. But Mother was sinking, becoming more feeble every day, unable to take solid food. That last night she wandered in her mind. 'I shall be seeing my little Emma soon . . . my little Emma . . .' 'Of course you will, Mother.' Elsie was watching by the bedside. There was no point in feeling upset because Mother had always wanted

Emma really. 'Oh . . . my little Emma,' she whispered, and closed her staring eyes.

Just before it was time to go to work, at the bleakest, coldest moment, Mother died. Elsie sat in the attic bedroom, feeling as lonely as Mother had said she would, like a ship without a rudder.

Funeral teas, ham, cakes and wine, all the ritual business of death kept her from brooding too much on the future. She was thirty-three years old now. What should she do? Enid announced that she would certainly become a nurse. That would leave Elsie alone in the house, without even a sister to look after. Where should she go? Mother, and Mother's illness, had shut her away from friends for years. Elsie had to bear some days of such thoughts before an unexpected visitor made her laugh as she opened the door.

Ralph had come back. Ralph Wilkinson from her school days, come journeying back from Cleckheaton as soon as he heard the news of Mother's death. He was a right one to make you laugh, and, just as he had done regularly when she was seventeen, he asked Elsie to marry him on the spot. 'I've waited, Elsie.' 'Aye,' she thought, 'we've all waited.' But the days of duty were over. She had nothing to do but agree according to her own wishes. She found saying 'Yes' difficult at first, though it was amazing how you improved with practice. 'Well,' said Ralph once it was all settled, without a note of complaint in his voice, 'it's been a long time coming . . . but it was worth waiting for.'

Lawrie Murfield
and the East Coast

The sea brings a different, almost foreign, flavour where it washes against such a proudly self-regarding land as Yorkshire. Fishing boats lost at sea, cargo ships sailing the world, lifeboatmen ever on call, these mix oddly with the artificial world of the seaside, the donkeys, grand hotels, fish and chip suppers, kippers and presents from Bridlington. Hidden from the rest of the wide inland world by the bare, wind-blown tops of the North York Moors, a scatter of fishing towns dug themselves into steep anchorages in the rocky coast: Saltburn, Staithes and Whitby. Further south the mixture of seaside became stronger as the towns had more space to grow and were easier to approach along the Derwent valley or over the Yorkshire Wolds and the flats of Holderness. Bridlington prospered there, and Filey, but above all, splendid Scarborough with its wealth of ornate stuccoed hotels, became the fashionable resort of Yorkshire's manufacturing rich.

Whitby was always a more serious and a poorer place, where fishing was a hard, necessary way of life. Lawrie Murfield was born to a fishing family in 1910, in a narrow yard down below the Abbey ruins, close to the harbour. There he learnt the skills of the sea, never ailing, never afraid, as he himself says, and something of a boaster into the bargain, as any fisherman should be.

A big-headed lad

December 16th 1914 began as an ordinary day. Mam
shouted up the stairs to him. 'Get up, Lawrie.' But he was
already moving. Lawrie would do his best to get anywhere
first, even when he was only starting at school and not
quite five. It was cold in that bedroom, so he pulled his
trousers on under the blankets. You could hear the wind,
even in the tight shelter of Blackburn's yard, but the gulls
were still mewing, so it couldn't be that wild at sea. A
fisherman's son learnt to scan the sky for signs of weather
almost as soon as he could speak. Now Dad was away in
the navy Lawrie was the man of the house and took his
responsibilities seriously. Mam called him her star of
heaven.

A grinning lad, young Lawrie Murfield, as he laced his
clogs and thundered down the bare, wooden stairs. 'Come
on, lad. Eat thy breakfast . . . look, there's Uncle Jack
home on leave.' The dripping tin was sizzling over the fire,
and Mam slapped a couple of slabs of bread into it. Uncle
Jack, with his boots off, was toasting the soles of his feet at
the bars. He had changed out of uniform right away into
his normal fisherman's jersey and trousers.

'Mornin', Lawrie,' said his uncle, 'I'll pour his tea,
Elizabeth.' 'Aye, do that . . . sit down lad, it's ready and
hot.' A man could grow well on bread fried in dripping.
Lawrie knew that. He had it every morning. First he
cocked his head at the window, seeing the early light, the
clouds streaming past, just checking in case he should
report a change of weather to the household. Then he blew
on his fingers, like his Dad, and picked up the fried bread.

'They say there's a German fleet out.' Uncle Jack was
talking over his tea. 'Is there now, I hope they're not
coming this way.' 'Aye, well, who knows . . . we should
have battened 'em in Kiel, by rights. But them officers in

London, they don't know a crab from a lobster!' 'They do say there's been submarines shooting at fishing boats down Grimsby way.' 'Oh, aye, they'll have to be watching out here in Whitby as well.'

Lawrie was listening with great attention to this war talk. His Dad and three uncles had all been in battle cruisers. Now, the *Hogue*, the *Aboukir* and the *Cressy*, had been sent to the Heligoland Bight to keep an eye on the German Navy. Those Huns wouldn't get far with Whitby men on the watch, even if Lawrie Murfield was a little young to do anything himself. He sat and wondered about the ships. How much bigger were they than keelboats or the steam trawlers that filled the harbours when the herring fleet was in? What was this German bite? When he'd finished his bread he could ask Uncle Jack. 'Come on, Lawrie darling. Get thy clogs on. Uncle Jack'll see thee to school.' 'Right Mam . . . but I wanted to ask about Germans.' 'Tha can chatter on t'way to school.'

Uncle Jack reluctantly pulled on his fisherman's boots and ventured towards the cold of the gallery outside the kitchen door. Stone steps led down into the yard and to the cellar where they stored crab-pots, oars and nets. Behind Blackburn's yard the east cliff rose steeply to the Abbey ruins high above, though cut off from their view by rows of cottages like their own, notched into the hillside, reached by a flight of steps. It was too steep for roads round that back end of old Whitby.

Grey and cold, they buttoned themselves tight and went down the flagged yard, through the narrow, whitewashed passageway and out into Church Street. Always lively, even on a grey December morning, was that street, and the old market place beside it, with its market stalls in front of the pillared tollbooth, and lassies in white aprons fronting their piles of provisions, winter vegetables, Christmas nuts, and the oranges that were a luxury in a fisherman's family. There Horsecarr Bull, the market butcher, yelled out his wares, while down the street came the smell of Johnson's celebrated pork shop, a delicious meaty aroma – compounded of roasting pork, baking pies, hot grilling sausages – mouthwatering even to a lad with a stomach full of bread and dripping. The memory of Johnson's pork pies hovered over many a longing Whitby fisherman as he sailed back from a hard night at sea. Then he would swear, like Lawrie himself, that the pies were so juicy, so succulent that there was no need to bite them at all, they simply dissolved in the expectant mouth of their own accord.

Lawrie passed Johnson's every morning on his way to school. The shop was dressed to suit the quality of its wares as, behind the crystal windows framed in carved and painted timber like Captain Cook's cabin, mounds of cooked meats rose artistically, capped with forests of sausages. Sometimes, just rarely, Mam would send him round for a pie or half a dozen sausage rolls, but not nowadays, not when Dad was at war and they only had his pay to live on.

At the corner of Bridge Street, facing the new, iron, swing bridge that separated the inner and outer harbours, you could look across to the other half of Whitby where the better-off folk lived and most of the holidaymakers stayed. The west side was much bigger, but not as old. It had the spa and the new hotels. But Lawrie's town was the old place 'over t'water', on the east, nestling under the Abbey, a huddle of narrow streets round the old market square, crowded tight against the harbour edge.

Uncle Jack left him at St Michael's School and he hid himself among the other lads in the bottom class, where they nudged and kicked each other with their clogs, keeping out of sight. The headmaster began prayers. All was still. Then an explosion shook the school. Prayers stopped. All the children waited. They could hear more explosions. The door burst open. 'Come on, out . . . get out.' Uncle Jack was with some other men. 'German ships out there . . . come on. They'll shoot again!'

After the first astonishment the school children were hurried outside and away from the danger. Along the side of the inner harbour they ran, among a crowd of fellow townsfolk from the east side, past shipyards and coal bunkers, past the seaman's hospital, over Spital bridge and along the banks of the River Esk, up Larpool Lane, jostling, panting, gradually becoming a confused, jumbled mob. Lawrie kept tight hold of Uncle Jack's hand and ran with the best of them.

Up at the top, past White Hall Wood, they all stopped, winded, then turned, drawn to watch the impending destruction of their town. Nothing less could be expected from those mythical Huns they had been hearing about in rumour, obviously quite different folk from the friendly German sailors they used to find, weeping drunk, in harbour. Clouds of smoke and dust were rising from around the Abbey buildings on the headland. As they looked northwards, towards the menacing sea, they could see the high skeleton of the old Abbey, the arched windows in the remaining walls, all silhouetted against the sky, then obscured for a while by drifting smoke. 'Why are they shooting at t'Abbey?' It seemed a daft thing to do, but St Hilda's Abbey was the symbol of Whitby. 'They're after t'coastguard station,' said Uncle Jack thoughtfully. The station stood on the cliff top, near the Abbey. 'Let's hope they don't go for t'shipping next . . . or there won't be much left of Blackburn's Yard.' Lawrie found himself wondering where Mam and the babies were.

The shelling stopped. They waited. It was cold and miserable up the valley, but safe. After a while, when nothing could be heard but the quiet buzz of speculation from all around them, news came that the German cruiser had sailed off. So Uncle Jack took Lawrie home, and there he found his mother and the babies safely drinking tea.

That was an exciting time to be a lad. The outer harbour was lined with grey, motor-torpedo boats in the place of cobles or keels. The larger, inner harbour, half a mile long or more as the Esk backed up at high tide, became a nest for seaplanes. Three of them, buzzing over the houses and around the cliffs, homing in on the Abbey ruins when they came back from the sea, were known affectionately as the bluebottle, redbottle and whitebottle. Lawrie and his mates speculated as to what adventures they had been on when they sputtered over the town to drift down onto the harbour. Perhaps it might be more exciting to fly a seaplane, your arms stretched out and buzzing as you ran down the steps, than to be skipper even of a motor-torpedo boat.

Mam had been very quiet for a while when news came that the *Hogue* was heavily damaged by torpedoes off Heligoland. Dad was missing. They had no news. Lawrie did his best to cheer her up, as a star of heaven should, but she had to wait for news of Dad. Eventually it came through that he was among the survivors, picked up and brought back to England. So were his three brothers and most of the other Whitby men. That was a blessing.

If it was traditional for Whitby men to join the navy in time of war, it was also essential for the next generation to learn their own trade. Lawrie was closely acquainted with the damp, fishy, stone-walled cellar that stretched under their house. He had played there since he was a baby, tangling skeins of nets, building towers of empty crab shells, trying out the hacksaw-like edges of lobster claws on his own fingers. Now he was old enough to begin to learn and make himself useful.

Dad, Uncle Thomas, Harry, Jimmy or William, his Uncle Jack, or old Graham from down the street, they all taught him at times, when they were on leave, or needed a sharp lad to help out. A fisherman's lad had a lot to learn. You began with baiting hooks, three hundred of them on a long cod line made up of twelve separate pieces. That had to be done in the evening, ready for a start before dawn next day. The slimy bits of old fish stuck to your fingers as you worked them onto the hooks, and your hands ached by the time a couple of lines were done. Until you got used to it.

Next it was making crab-pots, bending hazel boughs to the shape of arches and inserting the ends into a wooden base measuring twenty-two inches by nineteen. After that the side rods completed the cage, some of them being removable so that the catch could be got out. The tricky bit, the skilled work, lay in weaving the smouts which let crabs and lobsters in to get at the bait, but wouldn't let them out. Lawrie soon claimed to make pots as good as any lad, and better than many adults. Plant them anywhere against the rocks and you could reckon to hold a catch.

Other traditions came his way just as naturally as the fisherman's skills and lore of the sea that he absorbed with his bread and dripping. Every year, on the eve of Ascension Day, the whole school assembled along with most of the rest of Whitby, down by the water's edge of the inner harbour. It was generally sunny, as Lawrie remembers the day, with seagulls mewing overhead and a fine view of the west side, its jumbles of old, red-roofed houses rising up to the cliff-top plateau and the regular lines of stuccoed hotels.

Then they waited for the strange ritual to begin. It had to be at low tide, so the time of day varied, but always some men built a flimsy fence of interwoven sticks out on the sand whilst a big, fat man in black tail coat and tall black hat stood by, watching self-consciously. He was Mr Hutton, they whispered, and a fabulously rich landowner. When the fence was completed, standing on its own, absurdly erect in the sand, a man with a great horn would blow, loud and long, then make the ritual call 'out on ye, out on ye, out on ye!' That seemed to be it, for they all went slowly back to school, speculating about the penny-hedge, as the lads called it, though the headmaster always said its real name was 'the horn garth'. Lawrie's understanding was that if Mr Hutton didn't have it built every year, strong enough to survive three tides, he would lose his lands. Why that should be he had no idea, though when the tide was ebbing next morning they used to nip up before school to look at the penny-hedge, standing forlornly in swirling water, and wonder if it would survive and, if not, what would happen.

Whitby was that kind of town. It had an oldness and an oddness that you took for granted, like the queer ways of your grandfather. You didn't really inquire about them, they were simply there. All the tales of the Abbey, for example, its building and burning through history, simply went into a confused tangle of stories inside a lad's head. The German bombardment, of course, that was real and different. They all went up to look at the damage and to see if they could find fragments of shells. A pack of lads went racing up the hundred and ninety-nine steps to the cliff top, scavenging between gravestones of past sailors around the Parish Church of St Mary, stranded like an old ship high on the cliff top, to the great Abbey itself.

In those days Lawrie would wander away from his mates into the cliff fields and secretly lift a few turnips to return, bumping down the steps with a bulging sweater, the provider of his family. Mam was always glad to see a few turnips or carrots as the family grew, first Lawrie and Margaret, then George, Alf, Walter and finally Betty. A lot of mouths to feed even with free turnips, sweet to the taste, boiled, mashed and fried in dripping. Mam would send Lawrie back to the end of Henrietta Street, where the houses stank of fish-curing, to buy five pairs of kippers for a penny. They ate a lot of fresh fish at home, had to, and so kippers were a change, something more tasty.

Even when Dad came back, providing for a big household wasn't easy. Generally coal was short, and with the price at a shilling a hundredweight, they would buy it by the stone. You had to save up too long for a hundredweight. Still, there were always potatoes to be had cheap. You could get a houseful for a shilling, if you had it.

The main business of an eldest son in Whitby was to learn his trade as soon as possible, and to get to know that old enemy, the sea. Lawrie was rising remorselessly to the top class in school by the end of the war and able to go out regularly. Dad, on closer reacquaintance, proved to be a typical fisherman, strict when it came to discipline, as a skipper would require, superstitious, with a sixth sense that told him when to keep away from the sea and then helped him find who was holding the button when they bet against each other in the pubs. Dad was a strong man, rowing stroke oar in a Whitby boat that beat both Scarborough and Hartlepool. But he was not great businessman. Whitby fish buyers paid badly, but he wouldn't go round the corner to Scarborough with his catch to get a better price. He'd always sold to his mates, and he always would.

Dad had his own coble, the *Mayflower*, beautiful as her name. She was clinker built, as they all were, with a raked stern and flat bottom for easy launching from a beach. Cobles were fully ocean-going boats, generally around thirty foot in length, and carried a single mast. Whitby boats like *Mayflower*, were painted blue picked out in white. When the harbour was full of them, their tan sails up and the sun shining, it was a beautiful sight.

Lawrie had known and loved the *Mayflower* since he was a crawling baby. She was his playground above all else. He learnt to swim from shore to coble and back again almost as soon as he could walk. Unlike many sailors Lawrie was a good, and boastful swimmer. He was a lad who carried a fair amount of flesh, and, like a seal or some other aquatic animal, he was oddly buoyant in the water. It was almost as if, by some evolutionary process that laboured on Whitby fishermen, weeding out the unsuitable, favouring the survivors, Lawrie had emerged with an ideal physique. He found he could walk along in the sea with half his body unsubmerged, just treading water.

Given this peculiar advantage he would take his mates on at all kinds of watery challenges. They jumped from the swing bridge into the harbour. They raced the full length of the harbour mouth, past the grooved masonry blocks of the old west pier – with their hairy seaweed beards – to the end of the stonework, where Francis Pickernell's lighthouse towered above them with its windscoured doric columns. The next challenge was to swim on, out to sea, between the modern pier extensions, poor cheap timbers, compared to the massive nineteenth century stone pier. They would race to circle the harbour bell, then swim all the way back inside. Provided Lawrie won he was happy.

Dad trained him to sail, taking him out to sea regularly as soon as he was twelve. Lawrie had enjoyed school. He reached the seventh standard and at one time had dreams of educating himself up to qualify as captain of a ship.

That would have suited him well. But Dad couldn't possibly pay to keep him at secondary school. It had to be out after the fish as soon as the law would allow. That wasn't too bad, for Lawrie was bred and built for it and came to his full size and strength early. He was certain that he wouldn't remain a mere boat's lad for very long – on half shares only.

Trips to sea

By the time Lawrie was nearing his sixteenth birthday he was a fully-grown, solid lad, and powerful. Lawrie claimed he could smash any punch-ball at a fair with a single blow. He wasn't a boat's lad any more, but a working fisherman. When they sold a catch, one share went to the boat, one to old Graham, one to Lawrie, and half share to the lad. But Lawrie reckoned it was working for nothing at the price they sold fish. He wasn't intending to be a simple fisherman all his life.

A couple of steamship lines worked out of Whitby, so Lawrie went to see the agent of the Arrow Steamship Company. He knew the man, a whisky drinker, with a dirty, stained moustache and not much of a hold on his temper. 'Ah, it's young Lawrie . . . what dost'a want?' They all knew him in Whitby. 'I'm thinking of having a trip to sea.' 'Tha can't go till sixteen.' 'Aye, well I'm sixteen in a couple o' weeks.' 'Next ship's not due for six weeks, she's only bound for Hull.' 'Well, I might sign on, just to try . . . what's t'pay?' 'Four pound a month, all found.' 'Is that all?' 'It's all tha'll bloody get, young Lawrie. Tha'll take it . . . or take thiself to another bloody place.' Lawrie knew he was worth more than that. He'd show them!

So he went home, half decided to give it a try even at that miserable rate, and casually told his parents. 'I'm going to have a trip to sea . . . see if it's any different.' Mam looked at him slowly, and sighed. Dad nodded and blew on his dripping. Lawrie was his own master at sixteen, a working fisherman, and there was no way they could stop him, nor did they want to. They were used to a life where members of the family were away for a long or short time, somewhere at sea. You could always count on them coming back to Whitby. If they were still alive.

Lawrie took his first trip to Hull. It was easy enough work, and he went on to a series of coastal voyages, learning the seaways of the east coast from Edinburgh to Harwich. But he was only an ordinary seaman on four pounds a month wages, so when the salmon season came and he landed back in Whitby, he refused to sign on again. 'Well Lawrie,' said the agent, 'give another one a try. Captain Harley speaks well of thee.' But Lawrie, being independent, told him he had better things to do in the summer. He knew they would always want a good seaman.

Autumn brought an end to the salmon fishing and also brought high winds that kept Whitby fishermen ashore. One Sunday evening a gentleman, bowler hatted, a lady on his arm, penetrated the narrow entrance to Blackburn's Yard and climbed the steps to the gallery. A moment later Mam shouted inside, 'Lawrie, there's a man and woman here for thee.' Lawrie came out in his jersey and socks. It was Captain Harley and his wife. 'We're loading now, Lawrie,' said the captain, 'are you coming back with us?' 'Nay, I'm fishing with my Dad again.' Mrs Harley laid a hand on his arm. 'Come along, Lawrie, it won't be the same without you.'

Lawrie couldn't resist being needed, particularly by a lady. It went straight to his head. So he agreed to join the ship in Hull. She was a thousand ton, general cargo vessel, and he found her moored in Alexandra dock, loading sugar beet from sailing barges tied up alongside. They sailed from the Humber in December through mountainous seas, the wind northerly. Lawrie saw the Heligoland Bight, where his Dad had been sunk and rescued. The ship passed through the Kiel Canal and into the freezing Baltic. By desolate coasts, under leaden skies, they sailed along a narrow channel behind icebreakers to unload at Danzig.

When they returned to Newcastle, Lawrie was persuaded to sign on again, and this time they sailed in the opposite direction. For thirty-three days the screw never stopped as Lawrie was taken further from Whitby than he had ever expected. They crossed the Mediterranean to Port Said, then the Red Sea, to the Indian Ocean. At midnight the city lights of Bombay were glowing far out to sea. There they unloaded their mixed cargo, then sailed down the coast to Marmagao in the Portuguese colony of Goa, where they were to load ten thousand tons of monkey nuts.

Lawrie went ashore for a little while. He visited a fantastic temple covered entirely by carved monstrosities in gaudy colours brighter than any fairground at home. What interested him most was to decipher the signatures of fellow sailors scribbled on the walls, and see how many came from Whitby. He was also amazed by how the 'niggers' worked, shelling peanuts in the sun, hour after hour, under threat of a foreman's lath. No Whitby man would take it. Then they sailed for home, and Lawrie vowed he would never leave Whitby on a long voyage again. Travel wasn't for him.

Lawrie really loved his customary life as a fisherman, never afraid, very much his own master, free to boast of his catches when he came home. Sometimes he worked with his Dad, sometimes with old Graham. In the winter months they took *Mayflower* out to sea for up to ten miles, cod fishing with long lines. That was how Lawrie learnt to navigate back to Whitby harbour bell in fog and darkness from anywhere along the coast. March onwards was crabbing time. If you spent enough days and months planting two thirties of crab-pots among the rocks up and down you knew every individual cliff and submerged rock or reef at every level of tide from Redcar to Scarborough.

Salmon season was from June to August and then Lawrie worked with old Graham, casting six-inch mesh nets off the harbour mouth. They were required by law to keep at least fifty yards from the pier in order to let some fish up the Esk, to spawn in its headwaters on the North York Moors.

In August 1928 they had bad luck with the salmon fishing, always seeming just to miss the incoming fish when they had cast the nets. Hard work, long hours, and not much to show for it. One evening Lawrie and Graham had stowed their gear in the house cellar and were on the way back to the boat to collect some odd fish when the old man stopped, clutched Lawrie's arm and pointed silently. The harbour was alive with fish, jumping everywhere, all the catches they had never made, safe now from nets and free to go up-river.

Lawrie drew in his breath. 'We could go for 'em!' 'Nay, we'll get six months.' 'Come on, Graham . . . if we wait till dusk . . . there's fish for anyone out there.' They looked each other in the face for a moment, grizzled elder and plump-faced fair-haired youth. Eventually old Graham winked, slowly. Nothing more was said.

About nine o'clock, when it was getting good and dark, Lawrie rapped on Graham's door and they slipped down to the boat. The two of them crowded down inside her, hidden in the shadows, whilst the lad, Jack, made to row about the harbour a little. All around seemed placid and unwatching. They shot the nets as silently as they could, speaking in whispers, drew round in a tight circle and hauled in. Fish were there in plenty to be hauled on board, gasping, slithering cold in the hands. It was impossible to stay calm, unexcited and silent. 'We must have taken a hundred,' Lawrie crowed.

Satisfied with this one cast, they nudged Jack to row casually back to their moorings and crouched down again among the silver, writhing shadows of the fish. Jack tied up. They began to breathe again. Then a voice spoke from the quay above and they saw two stern pairs of boots before their faces, stolidly planted to prevent escape. 'Thomas Graham and Lawrie Murfield, eh?' 'Aye,' said old Graham shamefaced. 'We shall have to confiscate all the fish, and thy nets and boat gear. This'll go directly to the magistrates.' There was nothing to be said, only a silent, inwardly groaning, acceptance. Next day they were in court, sheepishly admitting their guilt. The bench fined them twenty-five pounds and five pounds costs for fishing in a prohibited area. Their catch was confiscated. It was a heavy blow in days when a good week's fishing would only bring Lawrie seven pounds, and some weeks brought in nothing at all.

A day's fishing had been wasted in this humiliating procedure, and now Lawrie stood beside the harbour again. Dusk was flooding in across the water as the sun, which had appeared for a moment below a blanket of low cloud, sank behind the buildings of the West town. Small patches of red flickered on the harbour surface in angled reflection from the sunlit clouds. Lawrie stared in amused anger at all this postcard beauty. You couldn't help but laugh. There they were again – more fish than ever, leaping about in the crowded harbour as if to taunt his impotence. Should they try again? No . . . it was daft. But then . . . the bailiffs would never, ever, suspect them that night. Not right after a day in court.

He ran up the alley, across Church Street, and banged on Graham's door. 'What is it now?' 'They're out again, jumping . . . harbour's wick wi' 'em.' 'Hast' gone daft?' 'Come on Thomas.' 'No!' 'Come and look, then.' 'Oh aye, I'll look . . . but nowt else.' They watched the fish jumping, and it became darker every second. There were thousands of them. It made you hold your breath just to watch. 'Go on, Thomas, just one shot.' He heard nothing, but felt an elbow in his side. In absolute, burglar-like stealth, they circled the harbour once, shot the net and hauled in. More fish even than the night before wriggled on the boards. Then they took the coble over to an empty mooring and hid her well away from the bailiff's normal path. Next morning they were outside the harbour mouth before dawn, and seen shooting their nets ostentatiously, well out to sea. When they came in they had a magnificent catch, one hundred and twenty fish. 'My, Lawrie,' said the buyer, 'that's a turn up . . . after yesterday.' 'Aye,' said Lawrie as he passed the money to Graham. It would pay the fine at least.

Thomas Graham's coble was called the *John Ray*, and she sailed well, especially when they took a westerly down to Robin Hood's Bay to fish for sea trout, passing by the black cliffs, the rocks and reefs famous for many a shipwreck. Lawrie would sit, upright at the tiller, holding the sheet and watching her tan sail fill with the wind, talking quietly to her: 'come on, lass.' The lee-side would be down, water creaming along the gunwale, as they hammered past the land, and old Graham would laugh. 'Look at him, that Lawrie . . . thinks he's skipper of the *Cutty Sark*.'

He loved that feeling, the boat under him, and himself holding her. That was real living. Then they'd spend all day among the rocks, work late into the night, and a big man like Lawrie, who needed his victuals, would begin to feel the night cold creep over him. They didn't take rum, couldn't afford it generally, but water or cold tea wouldn't quench your thirst or give you a bit of a feeling of warmth inside. A three gill bottle of home-made ginger beer, sweet and fizzy and almost chewy with ginger, that was quite something at midnight. You felt the hot ginger at the back of your throat, and the bubbles stirring your dry and sticky tongue. Ginger beer kept you going when the fish were scarce.

Lawrie reckoned he knew that coast so well he could find his way blindfolded to Whitby harbour bell from anywhere you cared to start him. He might be fishing, or doing the odd job as a seaman, it didn't matter. One day he sailed with Uncle Jimmy, who was skipper of the keelboat *Prosperity*, south from Whitby, bound for Hull. It came on foggy that night and black dark when they were only half a dozen miles out. You couldn't see your hand before your face. There was nothing to be done except try and stand to, wait for light, and hope. Tides were changing, currents might take them anywhere, and they were far too close inshore. Lawrie stood and listened to the close sounds of the waves echoing from the cliffs of that rocky coast. 'Watter's changing,' he warned his uncle, 'she's drawing to shore.' 'What's 'a mean?' 'She's drawing in, Jim . . .

look out for rocks.' A moment or two later they felt her shake and shiver. A shout came from the stern. 'She's touched! . . . Jim, she's touched!' 'Aye,' yelled Jim, and then it was all hands stand by to start the engine and try to get her off.

They managed to get clear and then hold her steady against the incoming tide, with a long wait still ahead before dawn. 'Dost' know where we are? I couldn't tell from here to Jericho,' shouted Jim. 'I know . . . we're underneath t'coastguard station . . . Robin Hood's Bay,' Lawrie shouted back, bellowing against the wind. Suddenly a voice interrupted from above the ship. Both jumped, but it wasn't the Lord. He wouldn't have a Yorkshire accent. 'I can hear thee, Lawrie Murfield . . . I can hear thee above 'em all!' It was the coastguard. Lawrie had been right, as usual!

Lawrie always claimed that he never ailed at sea, and had no fear, so it was natural enough for him to join the lifeboat crew, like most of his family and friends. There were days when the sky began to turn green, the wind freshened and no sensible fisherman would go out. Then the lifeboat cox'n would call them together. Uncle Harry was cox'n of the *Mary-Ann Hepworth* for most of Lawrie's time in her crew. If the sea came over the lighthouses, Harry would take stock of his oilskinned men and keep them together to await events. Then the news would come. 'There's one missing . . . it's the *Provider* . . . Storr . . . and he's making for Whitby.' 'It's going to be rough,' said Uncle Harry, 'he'll never get in here . . .' He looked over the crew's faces again. 'Anyone with a family here . . . if he don't want to go . . . I shan't blame him if he walks out . . . But we'll have to go if he comes inside Whitby Bay.' Nobody spoke. Nobody moved.

They waited, and the sea pounded against the piers and sweat built up under their oilskins. About three o'clock word came in over the radio from a North Sea trawler. They were standing by a fishing boat that had been forced to turn and run for Scarborough, she had lost three men. Ranks of Storr tombstones stood on the cliff edge of the graveyard, staring out to the sea where most of the family died. Now there would be more. The sea was still pounding at the harbour mouth. Harry waited till dark, but no call to action came. 'Right lads,' he said at last, 'time to stand down.' Lawrie climbed stiffly home. Most work was a matter of time and patience, of waiting and being prepared. Lifeboat service was no different.

Not surprisingly, when war came again in 1939 the Whitby fishermen were called into navy service. Lawrie had RNVR training, being paid two pounds a quarter to stay on, and when he was called up he was a cox'n with three badges. 'You're a wide bugger,' they said, and put him – which was surprisingly logical for the navy – into a minesweeper, a converted trawler, to work along the east coast that he knew.

Their ship was called the *Dorienta* and the holds were alive with rats and cockroaches. Lawrie was nearly arrested for inciting, the crew to refuse to sail until she was fumigated. But he managed to get his way without a court-martial and even agreed to consult the skipper in future. The skipper was a little man called Bill Reynolds. They had some fun and games in the early part of the war, sailing five times to Dunkirk. The last time they were shelled from the cliff tops by a German battery until they sailed hard inshore and steamed down the coast underneath the trajectory of the guns as far as Cape Nazaire. Lawrie claims he ran the ship 'from a corkscrew to a thimble' once they were back on the East Coast.

The minesweepers worked in pairs, carrying out long sweeps with wires slung between them. They used small charges slung from the sweep wire to blow mines loose. The charges were just powerful enough to blow off a man's finger. Lawrie would look out of the wheelhouse and see one of the crew dozing as he payed out the wire. 'Wake up.' His savage bellow would jerk the man rigid. 'You look right . . . you're bloody going to lose a finger!' The man's eyes would flicker into life for a while, then cold, fatigue and the mechanical work would begin to turn him drowsy again. They lost a fair number of fingers that way.

Now and then Lawrie got back to Whitby. He generally managed a few hundred cigarettes or some rum to sell and help out his family. That was the least he could do. But he was lucky to get as much as forty-eight hours leave at any time. If it was a Saturday he would take them to the Empire Cinema. Two minutes into the film and Lawrie would be fast asleep. Warm, quiet, out of danger, that was a Whitby man's natural reaction to circumstances. But it was a dreadful waste of a sixpence!

Bert Haley

in Cleckheaton

Cleckheaton was, of course, the centre of Bert's universe. Not much of a town to look at, perhaps, to outsiders, but set bang in the middle of the working parts of Yorkshire, conveniently close to Leeds, Bradford, Halifax, Huddersfield, Dewsbury, Wakefield and the legendary Heckmondwike. It had woods and fields nearby, where a lad could march with the scouts and camp and hide. Its working life provided hardships enough to force him to develop his own philosophy of life.

Bert was born in January 1903, an only son, and his mother feared he might suffer from soft bones, so she regularly went down to the lime-pit in Brook Street and collected pale-green lime-water from the spring below to give to her lad. Bert grew strong and tall enough. He watched red-coated volunteers parade through the streets of Cleckheaton, then saw the train take them away in khaki to their deaths in France. It all made him think, so that when he found his freedom he asked himself 'why me?' and was grateful.

Funerals

Bert saw it just after they moved to the top end of Brook Street to live with Grandad and Grandma. They had two bedrooms and Bert had to share the room above the shop with his mother and father. But he was only seven years old, so he went to his little bed in the corner long before they came up. Generally he was worn out by all his goings on, so it was straight up and straight to sleep. But this night he couldn't settle down. He tossed and turned, and looked at the black maw of the black iron fireplace which was just there, a darker patch against the night.

Grandad had been telling him about the ghost of a farmer, who had lived at the old place when it was a farmhouse and Cleckheaton was only a village, and had blown his brains out. Grandad's cheeks wobbled as he wheezed out the story, but Bert wasn't frightened, only interested. So he had gone to bed quite happy. Now he noticed a faint, blue circle of light on the wall above his bed. It seemed to be growing and then fading, pulsing in and out. Bert got out of bed, his feet cold on the boards, shirt-tails wrapped close round his thighs, and went to look out of the window. It might be the gas light in the street. But all he could see was an angle of Brook Street on a cold, winter night, the lamps shining dimly through curtains here and there, and a large bottle of coloured water in the herbalist's window across the way. So he went back to bed.

The light was still there. He couldn't close his eyes and forget about it. It waxed and waned, grew a little larger, then smaller, but not changing its regular pattern. Bert soon got used to it, and lay still, watching it sleepily, until it gradually took on the appearance of a blue face, a woman's face. 'I must be asleep', he thought to himself. So he reached up slowly and got hold of a hank of his hair. Then he pulled. The face was still there. His hand came away from his head. Bert was definitely wide awake. He looked at the face. It wasn't anybody he knew. It didn't seem to want to say anything to him. He watched it, lazily, for a while. Then he fell asleep.

Next morning his fingers were still clutching a handful of hair. He told his mother and father, and they laughed. Bert was never afraid of strangeness. As an only son he could go his own way, live his own life more than most children. He grew up to be more independent minded even than most Yorkshiremen, and never very happy to be tied to a slow and boring job. Bert enjoyed the rich and varied life around him in those childhood years before the First World War.

Their new home was not only an old farmhouse, with stone walls, stone-flagged floors, and a vaulted cellar beneath, but it was also a confectioner's shop. Grandma held a wine licence, and they also brewed beer in the cellar, where there was a draw-well hidden by a plank. You could see the water, black and deep-looking in the light of a candle held down the hole. When Grandma was brewing the strong smell of yeast filled the house. But the funerals fascinated young Bert particularly. A cortège would draw up in Brook Street, with carriages, horses with nodding, black feather-plumes, undertaker's men in black top-hats. Funerals were treated with due reverence in Cleckheaton. Then the mourners would file into the shop, to find all prepared for them. Rows of long-stemmed glasses filled with port wine, and the special funeral-biscuits, sponge, each shaped like a figure of eight, made in the kitchen for the occasion. Funerals were a profitable business for Grandad and Grandma.

Of course, they were not actually Bert's grandparents, though he called them that. Bill and Elizabeth Allard were actually his mother's aunt and her uncle by marriage. Mother had moved house to look after them because they were her closest living relatives. Grandad had the dropsy, he was so fat that he got wedged in armchairs and had to be hauled out. He weighed over twenty stone, and had special collars made for his great neck, collars that went round Bert's waist, and Bert was not a skinny lad. Grandad wheezed when he walked or talked and he was always swallowing, gulping air like a fish. It made mealtimes a bit of a spectacle. He still kept his long, copper trumpet, and loved brass band music, but he couldn't play much as he got worse. He had no wind. And Grandma wasn't much better, because her bones were crumbling inside her. Bert knew this, and with a lad's concept of the human skeleton it fascinated him to think of it. She was all bent over, it pained her to move at times, but at least her case was a rare one, and she got special treatment in Leeds. They were both kind enough to Bert. Grandad still worked as an undertaker's joiner, which was a good connection for the funeral trade.

Bert explored the house thoroughly, first the beer barrels in their stone niches in the cellar, then up the steps to the kitchen, where the cooking and baking for the shop went on. There were wooden bins for flour and sugar, and working slabs of beech and marble for rolling out pastry. Bert used to clamber up on the marble slabs when he heard squealing in the evenings, and push with his hands on the under-drawing until he felt the baby rats stirring in their nest. 'Get down. Get them boots off my clean marble,' his mother would say. She was a Kenworthy, come down in the world, but still with remote but wealthy relatives. One uncle had died in the hunting field, and her father was a gentleman-joiner who committed suicide. So mother insisted on cleanliness and proper behaviour, as befitted their station.

Bert went off to explore the loft, where he could involve himself in cobwebs and dust to his heart's content. There he found a boy's treasure trove. It was an old, leather trunk with a tin lining. Grandad told him later that it had belonged to a sailor who was buried at sea. So Bert delved through the rope-ends, the bits and pieces that filled the trunk, his imagination glowing brighter with the dim light that filtered into the loft. At last his hands closed on something tangible that fitted his thoughts. It had a long, black-painted stem, with a plaited basket at each end. The baskets held lumps of lead, pear-shaped, one large, one small, and there was a loop of leather at the small end. What kind of navigational instrument could this be? Bert took it downstairs in triumph. 'Where have you been, Bert?' Mother exclaimed, shaking her head. 'What a state! What have you got there?' Bert held up his trophy. Grandad chuckled and wheezed from beside the kitchen fire. 'Why, it's a shillelagh, a real Irish shillelagh, as I'm a Christian.' He took the club from Bert and whirled it menacingly in the air.

The shop bell rang. Life was always punctuated by the shop bell. It was the yeast-man, basket over his arm, the yeast protected by a cover of waterproof American cloth, like fine tarpaulin. He had his hand-scales in the basket, and mother bought yeast for the next week's baking. Then it was the oatcake man. They rarely baked their own oatcakes. These were good and cheap, and a supply of the flaps generally hung on the flake in the kitchen. Meanwhile Bert was able to escape into Brook Street where he was never short of fascinating things to become involved in.

Brook Street ran up from Cleckheaton, and their house was at the top. The manufacturing town was a kind of microcosm of all that went on in the West Riding of Yorkshire at that time. It lay in the middle of that prosperous, self-congratulatory manufacturing area, first fruit of the industrial revolution, surrounded by Leeds, Bradford, Halifax, Huddersfield, Wakefield and Dewsbury. Cleckheaton had skills of all kinds, but mostly connected with textiles or engineering. It was all part of Bert's life. He grew up knowing that the man in a greasy smock who had just passed him was a wire-drawer, because of the reek of sour beer-grounds they used to quench the red hot wire. He knew all the girls from Sugdens, the shirt-makers down Brook Street. They thought themselves a cut above the mill lasses, did those shirt-rivers, because theirs was clean work. They didn't need to wear clogs and shawls to go to the mill. But they earned less for their gentility, twopence half-penny for a finished shirt, and had to pay for hire of their sewing machines and for broken needles. But those lasses wouldn't have gone elsewhere.

Cleckheaton was not the sort of sprawling city that cuts a boy off from open air and the countryside. Like so many of the smaller manufacturing towns, it had hills around, and open countryside at the end of the streets. Bert always loved the open air. He liked to get out and away from crowded folk. Two miles out of Cleckheaton he could be eight hundred feet up and looking down on his home. Only ten miles away to the west you were in the high, desolate moorlands of the Pennines, right in the heart of Howarth, where Emily Brontë wrote *Wuthering Heights*. Bert could never resist the hills.

He didn't need other people, though he liked to watch their odd ways. Perhaps that was with being an only son. He was very fond of his Dad, Lamplough Haley, a quiet-spoken, self-respecting man, who never raised his voice, a right counsel of a chap, as they called him. Lamplough loved his music. He had joined Grandad's Victoria Brass Band as soon as he was old enough, and now played second cornet for the Bradford Philharmonia. He even became a member of the Volunteers so that he could play in their band, though he wasn't in any way a military man. He had a weak heart, and no thought of fighting anyone. The Colonel of the Territorials had been heard to say of Lamplough's band, 'They may be fine players, but they're bloody rotten shots.' So Lamplough would appear in front of his admiring wife and son in a bandsman's scarlet coat, silvered helmet, white trousers and white-pipeclayed belt, his cornet under his arm. Then he would sneak out of the house, and across the fields, and dodge up to the drill hall the back way. He didn't like to be seen in his uniform.

As soon as Bert was old enough his Dad bought him a cello, but it proved a lasting disappointment, for Bert never got on. He never could get to practise. As soon as anyone knocked on the door he wanted to be off and away. 'Are t'coming, Bert?' and that was it. Dad was a good mechanic, an engineer as they called them, and a craftsman. He had begun work at Blakeboroughs in Brighouse, grinding valves, but now he worked at a timber-machinery concern in Cleckheaton, making power-saws, grinding lathe-beds, cutting decorative scrolls in the metal. Bert aimed to follow his Dad and become an engineer in time.

But not yet, there was too much going on in Cleckheaton. Every year they had the fair, on the Feast field down Peg Lane. A proper fair, with brandy-snaps, pie and peas, fairground organs played by punched paper, steam swings and hissing kerosene lamps spreading a reddish glow. One year they had that newfangled thing, a cinematographic representation, where Bert paid his penny, climbed to a seat through a painted model of a railway engine boiler, and then sat, gripped with excitement, as he was whirled through the countryside, apparently seated on the very front of the engine, with objects rushed towards him at terrifying speed. That was really something new. But he had also helped his friend, the herbalist, fill two washing-baskets full of bottles with coloured water in them, to be sold at the fair as an infallible cure for the rheumatics. 'Only sixpence a bottle, Madam . . . I have a letter here from a gentleman in Huddersfield who will guarantee the efficacy of the preparation . . .'

Among the other sideshows was a 'Professor of Mathematics', in real cap and gown, who gave amazing demonstrations of mathematical skill, calculating square roots, cubes, rapid multiplication or division with astonishing speed, and offering for sale a booklet that gave the secret of his success. Bert wasn't tempted.

He would go to the fair along with Uncle Handel, who played the trombone like a man inspired. All father's eight brothers played some instrument, which was why there was so much disappointment over Bert's cello, but Uncle Handel was the best. Uncle Handel used to practise in Church Street every Sunday morning and welcome the folk out of church with a rendering of the March from the *Mastersingers*. A more profitable business had opened to him because of his skill. A tooth-drawer used to practise at markets and the fair. He had an arrangement to borrow a coal-merchant's flat-cart at weekends, and this he decorated with a large red and white banner, 'Painless Extractions'. Uncle Handel was hired as an extra attraction and he would play a rousing tune to draw the crowds. The first sufferer would take his seat, out would come the iron calipers, to be fastened on the offending tooth. The drawer would take a breath, tense his muscles . . . and wink at Uncle Handel. To a blast of the trombone that drowned any possible screams, the tooth was drawn. Nothing more painless could be imagined, and Uncle Handel earned his beer money.

Bert had other sources of amusement when fairs and markets were off, and there were no street entertainers in town, no performing bears or German bands. He joined the boy scouts, and his mother put together a magnificent uniform for him, from broad-rimmed hat to gartered stockings. Bert loved the scouts, the country exercises and the camps. He had his heroes among the older boys, the pack leaders who went on twenty-four hour marches and covered miles over the hills. He could listen to their talk for hours and planned to emulate them. Because of his pleasure in being a scout he actually found the self-discipline to learn to play the bugle in a reasonable fashion. The family's musical tradition came to hand as soon as he tried. He hardly ever seemed to be at home.

There was school, of course, but Bert didn't think a great deal to that. He got two inch splinters in his backside from wriggling on the roughly planed benches, and his Dad had to remove them with a pair of tweezers. He was forever spitting on his slate and wiping it clean with the heel of his hand to start again. They had one Scotch teacher, ex-army, who was six foot tall and terrified the boys. When he was only in standard four Bert would watch in terror through the glass partition as the cane was slowly raised above that teacher's head, shaken dramatically, swished in the air once or twice, and then brought down on the culprit's fingers. He didn't want to get on in the school if it meant rising into that class. But he didn't play truant, because you were beaten on your backside in front of the school.

When he couldn't get out on a wet winter's evening, Bert would sit quietly in the kitchen and look at the paper for a little while. He was growing up, ten years old. He'd be a working man in a couple of years. 'Bert,' said his mother. 'Aye, mam.' 'Go and fetch old Mrs Schofield, lad. There's a telegram I want to show her.' So Bert went down the street and knocked on old Mrs Schofield's door, and peeped inside. She was old all right, spoke so broadly there were words he couldn't understand. Her old man had been a teamer, handling horse-drawn waggons. He tied his breeches up with string and always smoked a short, yellow, clay pipe upside down – to keep out the rain. Old Mrs Schofield used to dry tea leaves to mix with his twist tobacco and make it go farther. They had lived through hard times, those two, and they slept together in a box-bed in the kitchen, the iron kettle on the fire, day and night. Bert gave his message and went back home.

Shortly afterwards old Mrs Schofield came in. She looked around and saw Bert. 'Nay, lass,' she said to Mother, 'ain't that right clever, yon lad reading t'paper.' Mother had the telegram in her hand. 'Now, Jenny, do you know what this is?' 'Nay, I don't.' 'It's a telegram.' 'Then, where's t'hoiles?' 'What do you mean, holes?' 'How do they get it on t'wire, then, wi'out hoiles?' Bert and his mother looked at each other in amazement. Mother decided not to try and explain. Bert went back to his paper.

The old generation were going fast. It was January 1914, and Bert was eleven years old. Grandad had died of his dropsy. He was too big to get down the stairs, so they took out the bedroom window and frame and swung him down on a block and tackle. They had the funeral tea at the shop.

Grandma was crumbling worse and worse, her back bent over like a witch. She dreaded going to the Leeds, to the theatre of the medical school, with all those students watching her as doctors examined her. Her death was a merciful release. That night Bert crept up the staircase with his candle and looked into Grandma's room. She was lying out on the bed, as straight as could be expected. He went softly over to her and stood, staring at her face in the candlelight. It was stiff and hard, so he ran his hands over the cold flesh, just to see, then went across the landing to his own bed.

Forget-Me-Nots

The First World War began with a bang and the sound of music as far as Bert was concerned. It was exciting, the stuff of adventures, to see the military bands, his Dad playing among them, with red coat still, and the moving columns of recruited men passing through the town. The war would be won in six months, all the lads knew that, and they envied the older ones who would be in at the victory. Men joined up from every sort of trade, leaving the humdrum settled routine they had brought themselves to expect for the rest of their lives, a pattern like their fathers', to face open air, change, foreign parts, and death. Bert and his mates cheered them wildly. Wasn't Mr Hurst, the scout leader, their great hero, marching off to victory, whilst they were left behind.

But the war dragged on into 1915 and 1916 and the troops were stuck in khaki and the trenches. There was talk of conscription, as the first enthusiasm died with its volunteers. Bert left school at thirteen and found a lad's job, helping at a small stationers and printers. There he had every odd job to do, starting at six with the paper round and ending at half past five after chopping firewood for the proprietor and rolling firelighters out of waste paper for the shop ladies. He was paid six shillings a week.

He did also have an opportunity to learn, for at times he had to help out with the printing. Bert was too short to reach the machine without standing on a buffet, but he learnt to print visiting cards, spreading the ink with a palette knife onto a marble slab, then inking the gelatine roller. He had to work two handed, blank card in, printed card out, to the rate of the machine, and each card must be lined up exactly against a couple of drawing-pins stuck into the base as guiders. They were very particular at the shop.

It was even more of a business making cards for the Territorial Officers Ball and the Conservatives Ball. Then he must stop the machine after each batch, whilst the ink was still wet. He took them down to the cellar, lit by the dim watery light that filtered through thick panes of glass set into the pavement and down a splayed, white-tiled, light shaft into the room. There was kept a bag of gold dust, and it was Bert's job to shake the wet cards in this bag, so that the lettering turned to gold. Dust made the cellar 'all tinkling with gold', and the cards came out looking grand, but it was said to be bad for the health, and when he was doing it Bert was supposed to drink a pint of milk every hour. After the cards were gilded he had to punch a hole in one corner and tie on a small pencil with silk cord. Then the ladies were properly equipped to write the names of their partners for a waltz or schottische.

Bert didn't mind doing the printing, he rather liked the twinkling of gold dust. It was a different matter with the Church magazines. He had to fold every one, as it came off the press, with a bone rod so as not to dirty it. Then he had to deliver them, loaded onto a flat wheelbarrow. They weighed a ton, and he was not a big lad. So Bert salvaged the raffia rope that came round the orange boxes, tied it to the barrow handles, and hung part of the weight round his neck. That helped, but it was still hard going – uphill to the Church at Robertown – miles and miles it seemed with the iron tyres rumbling over paving setts and his arms stretching as he went.

Bert was sitting on the wooden seat of the lavatory in the backyard behind the shop one day when he heard the explosion. The noise was like a thunderclap, and at first he thought the yard wall had fallen down, so he sat tight. It wasn't his fault. Then he heard his Dad's voice in the passageway, 'Come on lad . . . Low Moor's going up!' . . . Another explosion followed, with a volcanic cloud of debris rising in the air from over the hill where the munitions works was burning. 'By! It's all going up!' They heard galloping horses and turned to look as the Cleckheaton fire-engine set off towards the flames, brave in brass helmets and red buckets. It was over the hill in minutes, speeding down towards Low Moor. The men watched for a moment, hearing more explosions. Was that a red bucket amongst the smoke clouds? Had men and horses all gone? It was just like war. Parts of the engine were later found miles away in Heckmondwike. Two firemen survived.

Bert slipped behind his Dad and ran for home. On the way he saw their doctor, black bag in his hand, walking steadily uphill towards Low Moor, ready to do what he could. Bert nipped into the house through the back door, washed his face – he knew his mother would stop him otherwise, took his bike and set off to see the fun. He didn't want to miss anything. Fortunately the explosions weren't stopping yet. He could still hear one every now and then. Over the hill he came on something like hell – burning, smoke, blackened streets, ruined buildings, the sky darkened, the noise of sudden explosions unnervingly close. Not like the glamour of war at all. In his excitement Bert pedalled closer.

Bert was in time to see the gasometer go up. The huge, iron cylinder seemed to peel apart like a banana. Then the gas inside it rose majestically in the air like an airship, still in its cylindrical shape. It hovered for a moment. Then it blew. Bert was stunned by the sound and sight. For a moment he crouched for shelter beside a broken-windowed house. Then he walked nearer. He didn't want to miss anything. A policeman saw him. 'Hey, lad! Get down there!' He pushed Bert back down an alleyway and into the backyard of a house, where he was made to lie down with other refugees. This was no fun at all, nothing to be seen. So Bert sneaked out again, but by now there were policemen everywhere and he could get no nearer to the display. He recovered his bike and went home. It had really been something to remember.

His mother was far too busy to notice the state he was

in. 'Come on Bert. Where's tha been? There's help needed.' He looked out at Brook Street. It was like the stories they had heard from France. A column of refugees, mostly on foot, shambling along, shocked and blackened, some pulling hand-carts piled up with their household goods, coming from all the area round Low Moor. Mother set Bert to work taking chairs out into the yard as she set the biggest iron kettle on the fire. Soon they were serving tea to these distraught and weary folk. The full tale of dead and wounded took some days to complete.

Bert and his mates had awesome experiences to compare, for weeks to come. Few of them had dared to go as close as Bert. Then the excitement died, and ordinary wartime news came back. Mr Hurst was dead. That was strange, for heroes shouldn't die, and other senior scouts had left the troop to go to war. They were far from Cleckheaton and might be suffering all kinds of hardship. The war didn't seem to be about to end that year. Somehow the idea came, that the scouts would set up a fund to send out home comforts to their own folk. What should it be called? Why, of course, the 'forget-me-not fund'. They set to with a will. Bert went round the mills, selling coloured cards impregnated with 'famous scents' at a penny a card to the factory girls. On a good day he might sell fifty, and that was four shillings and twopence for the fund.

After Low Moor the troop had built up their track-cart with detachable ladders on the side, so that they wouldn't be left out of any emergency. Now they went round with it from door to door, collecting old bottles, jars and glassware to resell. They stored their loot in the scoutroom, and it was when doing the storing that Bert had a half pound of mustard-coloured piccalilli sauce spilt over his best uniform. And mother could say nothing. It was all in a good cause.

He stuck the printing job for about a year, until one of the lads got on to him at scouts one evening. 'How much are t'gettin, Bert?' 'Six shillings.' 'I can get thee more'n that.' 'Where?' 'Just come wi' me to Jas Smith's.' So Bert went to Jas Smith's, the dyer, and they paid him ten shillings a week, which wasn't bad at fourteen. But he disliked the job. They put him onto war work, cleaning old uniforms that came back from France, mostly German. Some of them proved to be the khaki aprons issued to highlanders to protect their kilts from the mud of the trenches. They were bloody, torn, with bullet holes and burn marks. After the first interest in what it all meant, this rather got Bert down.

It wasn't helped by the old heroes coming back from the front, sometimes arriving at scouts in just such uniforms as he was handling, covered in mud. Some had been wounded, had lost an arm or leg, and wouldn't be much good for work ever again. Bert met them at scouts and looked at them with older eyes. Many of them had learnt to wind wool into long, coloured ropes over four pins stuck into a bobbin whilst they were convalescing. 'French knitting' they called it, and Bert used to take round the finished lengths, wound into circular table mats and such, to sell for the fund. But it didn't go well. What use could folk make of it?

The war had been dragging on for almost three years when Bert got his chance of a proper job. There were very few carding machine tenting businesses in the world, for it was a skilled and complex job constructing the machines that made the wire cards that were used in wool-combing. Delicate machinery was used, more like clockwork than anything Bert had seen at his Dad's works. Generally speaking they didn't have vacancies at that shop. Jobs were kept in the family, and no-one else stood a chance. But now many of the apprentices had gone to join the army and they were short-handed.

Bert went in cautiously his first morning. Everything was clean, dusted, the machinery moving smoothly, and his Mother had provided him with a white apron as instructed. That was quite something, a white apron for work. A big man was sitting in a corner, reading a paper. Bert went over to him. He was the foreman. He looked at Bert rather coldly over the top of his newspaper, then indicated a jar of light machine oil with a feather in it.

'Right. Tha can start by going round wi' this. I'll show thee what to oil . . . and don't put much on. We don't run trams here.'

Bert did the oiling, carefully, as instructed. He wanted to go to the lavatory, so he asked one of the men. No answer, he just turned his back on Bert and spat. Bert went round with the oil feather again. Then it seemed to be time for tea, so he asked someone else. Again, the man didn't answer, just ignored him and walked away. This went on all day, and Bert felt more and more miserable, for he was always a cheerful, friendly, talkative lad.

His Dad was waiting when he got home. 'Nah then, how've you gone on, lad?' 'I didn't like it, Dad.' 'Oh,' said Mother interrupting quickly, 'you're not used to being in a mill . . . that's what it is. You're used to being outside . . . it'll take time, that's all.' Bert nodded. He was a bit shaken by his first day. Tuesday was the same, and Wednesday. He began to dread the thought of Thursday as soon as he got home. After tea there was a knock at the door, and he went to answer it. There stood the manager of the works. Bert stared. 'Is your Dad in?' said the manager. Dad was already coming. 'What's he been doing?' asked Dad.

But the manager took off his hat and came inside, and they all sat down together. What he had to say was more like a committee resolution than ordinary conversation. 'Now then, Mr Haley, I've got to tell you that the men have come to a conclusion, and I can't oppose it. They say we shouldn't employ another apprentice until we know if the old lad wants to come back after the war. It can't be long to go now, and I can't promise work for two of them . . .' A silence whilst this sank in, and Dad nodded in understanding. Then the manager added, 'You'll have to withdraw him.' There was nothing more to say, so he stood up, took his hat and left.

Well, it didn't worry Bert half as much to be unemployed as to go back to that unwelcoming place. His Dad found him some temporary work, and Mother gave him back five shillings a week pocket money, so he was still better off than most of his mates. Then, just over a month later, the manager returned. He explained that they had now had a letter from the old apprentice, who said he was enjoying army life and didn't want the job. Under the circumstances it was only right that Bert should go back.

Bert wasn't that worried, but his parents pointed out the advantages of getting a proper apprenticeship and becoming a skilled man. It could set you up for life. But it still felt a cold place. They sent him for spells in all the departments, the planing shop, turning, fitting. But everyone was suspicious, afraid to teach anyone else in case they lost their job. Bert would stop to watch someone in the turning shop cut a fine, decorative scroll on a piece of machinery. It was beautiful to watch. Then the man would turn and glare at him. 'What the hell dost'a want? Clear off!'

He signed his article of apprenticeship all the same, and next day they told him to come down to the boiler house at dinner time. He knew why, but it was no good keeping away. So Bert put on a brave face, and found it not too bad. They simply hauled off his trousers and daubed him all over, liberally, with heavy oil before shaking quantities of coal dust over his private parts. It was a good job his mother knew what to expect. Even then she was cross, mostly with Bert, which seemed unfair, but also with men in general.

That night he went to choir practice, and, when they had a break and went outside to the back of the wall, he showed the lads what had been done to him. One friend, newly apprenticed at the P & M Motorcycle Firm, shook his head in amazement and said, 'They don't do that at our place.' Bert was surprised to hear it, less surprised to be taken aside at the next choir practice by the same friend. It was true. They didn't do that at his place. They had painted him with black lacquer instead.

Bert was fifteen by then, the war still wearily continuing, with no prospect of an end. It seemed as if their whole generation might have to go out and fight when, each in turn, reached conscription age. Meanwhile Bert still went to the scouts, and, with a simpler instrument than the

149

cello, had become a star bugler. Old heroes were still dying in the trenches. News came, and sometimes, even, their bodies were sent back for burial at home. Then Bert stood by the graveside in his scout's uniform and played the last post for them. There was nothing more he could do.

Fit for Heroes

They were still coming back. Bert used to go to meet them at the station when he could get away after work. Sometimes there were bands playing, but a lot of men had gone to war, and most of his early heroes were already disposed of. The bands sounded cracked and hollow without them, and without his Dad playing, for Lamplough Haley was increasingly unwell and Mother was worried.

The Great War to End All Wars was over. Only the echoes rumbled on, like slow explosions, as the heroes returned. Some came home maimed in body or mind. Others were apparently unharmed, needing only to adjust to ordinary working life right away. If the work was to be had.

Bert could feel things getting colder and tighter all the time at work. He was doing a man's job, though paid as an apprentice, for the wartime boom in all engineering had forced them to make use of anyone they could. If the lad could do the job, that was it. He hadn't stayed in the card-making machinery shop, but moved about the general engineering sections of the firm.

Now it seemed back to when he first started, in atmosphere at least. Trying to find out how to cut a double-screw, he watched one old craftsman whirling the spirals of cut steel away as easily as if he were unpeeling elderpith. Then the man stopped, spat tobacco juice accurately from the wad he was chewing onto the end of his cutting tool. It hissed and stank sourly. He turned a grizzled, bristling chin to Bert, who was watching fascinated. 'What's wi' thee?' 'I need to learn double-screwing.' The old man waved the tool at him. 'Find yer own bloody way . . . Clear off before I thump thee!'

They took on a new man as a fitter. Back from the war he came, with hair cropped and brushed smooth, well-shaven, more smartly-dressed than you would expect a fitter to be, desperate for the job. Half-way through Monday morning the manager came and stood at the cross-roads in the fitting shop, looking round. The new man was working with hammer and cold chisel, and the manager's eyes fixed on him. He was working with his right hand half-way up the hammer. No fitter who had been properly apprenticed would do that. You couldn't strike a decent blow. 'You're no fitter,' said the manager. The man looked up. He went white, but said nothing. 'Out!' That was that.

Discipline was tight enough in the works. No chatting allowed in working time, no horseplay, even from the apprentices, and you had to work right up to the buzzer. No clearing away in advance was allowed. Only occasional brawls brought any change to this dull routine.

On Armistice Day all work stopped, for the two minutes silence in memory of those who had died in the war. The first anniversary was a solemn occasion. By the time of the second the interest of lads who had never fought was waning. They were tired of war heroes. A young appren-tice, rather a cocky lad, sat next to Bert. On the other side was a man who'd been in the trenches, won the Military Medal, and come back to work. He was not that old, only about twenty himself. That day the buzzer went for silence. The belts flapped, slowing down as power was cut off. The machines rolled to a halt and all was quiet. Then the cocky lad began to tap with his hammer on his bench. The old soldier stood at attention by his lathe and ignored him. He stood there for the full two minutes, and his eyes never moved.

The belts started up again. The period of silent respect was over. That was it. The ex-soldier vaulted Bert's lathe, pulled the cocky lad to his feet and knocked him down

151

again. He dragged him across to the pile of swarf, metal cuttings, filings, sharp-edged waste pieces and rubbed his face hard into it. Then he let him go, bleeding and crying, to wash off the blood and creep away home. Neither foreman nor manager said anything about it.

Four years passed after the war, it was 1922, and business was getting no better, for Yorkshire engineering at least. Bert was nineteen, still apprenticed, and finding life harder altogether. Dad had fallen ill, with his weak heart – that kept him even from cornet playing. 'Angina,' said the doctor, 'he can't last more than a few weeks . . . and I'd give my right arm to save him. He's a perfect gentleman is Lamplough.' As always, Bert's quiet, inoffensive Dad did as was expected of him. He died in due time, and they held the funeral at the shop.

Bert wasn't at all ready to be man of the house. He had relied on his Dad's counsel, on the peaceful way he managed the household, his strong beliefs and acceptance of the world as it was. Bert didn't really want the responsibility. He was only paid as an apprentice, and took an apprentice's view of life. The next blow came fast. It came as a knock on the door one evening. Bert opened it to a small, dapper man. 'Hello,' said Bert, not knowing him. 'I'm Mr Bamford,' said the man, 'I've bought this shop.' This was the first either Bert or his Mother knew of it, but it proved to be true, and Mr Bamford had bought the freehold with the intention of opening a fish restaurant on the site. He didn't want tenants, however long established. They had a month to leave. That was that.

They found a house to rent. It bothered Mother more than Bert. After all she was a Kenworthy, and he was a happy sort of lad who didn't worry. Of course, they lost the income from the shop, and they couldn't eat their own goods anymore. So Bert, the bread-winner, persevered at his engineering apprenticeship. By 1924, when he was just twenty-one, Bert was about at the end of his seven years, almost a skilled man.

Work was still scarce. Employers were talking of cutting wages. Bert was now working with a group of lads in the turning-shop. Management was down on them particularly, and had threatened to sack the lot if there was any more horseplay. One eighteen-year-old lad had recently been killed when he was caught in the lathe by his clothing, swung round and up, so that his head was smashed on a beam. You could see where his brains had splattered. They worked on big, powerful, metal-turning lathes in that shop.

All of one morning, whenever no supervisor was about, the lads had been throwing greasy cloths at Bert. He had pretended to ignore them, but by dinner-time he had a pile a foot high by his bench. 'This can't go on,' he said to himself, 'or the lad's 'll think I'm duffin.' So after dinner he bent down, picked up the top rag and threw it at his chief persecutor. No sooner had he done it, then a roar came from the drawing-office, which was a half level higher than the shop. 'Haley! Come here!' The foreman had seen him. Bert went up, sheepishly. He couldn't really say anything in defence or they'd all lose their jobs. 'You'll leave at the end of the week.' Bert went back to his bench.

The faces of those lads! They knew what it meant. Bert reckoned he was out of work for life. But there was no malice in them, only fun and games. After work they collared the foreman, all together, and told him what had happened. It wasn't Bert's fault at all. Even a foreman might be human. He relented, and Bert was reinstated.

A couple of weeks later, Bert was given a dynamo pulley to turn for a passenger train. It came up from the forge as a really bad casting, full of blowholes and carbon black. He groaned when he saw it. 'Get it done by dinner-time,' was the verbal instruction, 'they need it right away.' The ticket on it had become so scuffed, dirtied and torn on its way up that he could barely read it. 'Eight inch, by eight inch, by inch and a quarter hole', was how Bert deciphered the dimensions to himself. It was a bit doubtful, but, not daring to leave his lathe to ask, he set about turning it.

Well, it was a real bastard, that casting, but Bert got it turned to a smooth, gleaming cylinder and sent it off for checking. The foreman came back with it, his face like a heap of swarf, blank and bristling. 'What the hell's this?' He showed Bert the ticket. 'Aye, eight by eight by one and a quarter. I've done it.' 'No you bloody haven't! Can't read?' He thrust the label in front of Bert's nose until he could just make out the smudged remnants of a figure after the second eight. 'They wanted this eight by eight and a quarter. Now it'll have to be done again . . . a new forging and the lot . . . There's no room for thee here . . . not wi' bad work done. Leave on Saturday, and don't come back!'

Bert stood by his lathe. It really was the sack this time, and he knew it. It had happened before, lads losing their jobs just before they finished their apprenticeship and must be paid a man's wage in future. There was always some reason given, 'bad work' or something. But you knew. By rights he should have been angry, but he only had a sick feeling in his stomach. He'd have to tell his Mother.

Bert was by no means the only one. It was the same tale everywhere, and it grew worse year after year. When you were on the dole you hung about, lost. Sometimes you went scrattin on the coal tips to find a bit of fuel. Bert spent whole days digging over the shale with his hands to come back with a small bag of bits that smouldered coldly in the grate. There seemed no hope for him. He hadn't even finished his apprenticeship, and there were skilled, experienced men after the same jobs.

They gave him sixteen shillings a week, and his union fund made it up to eighteen. Every now and then the local committee called him in for questioning before them, standing in front of a deal table with the black telephone at the secretary's right hand. 'Now, Haley.' 'Yes sir.' 'How long is it since you applied for a job?' 'Yesterday.' He couldn't keep on saying, 'sir', even under those circumstances. 'Oh? Where?' 'I walked to Halifax.' 'And where did you go in Halifax?' 'I went to Asquiths – th'engineers.' 'I see . . . and what time did you go?' 'It'd be about eleven o'clock when I got there.' 'Would it?' The chairman nodded to the secretary, who picked up the phone and rang Asquiths. 'Has a man called Haley been to you for work? . . . I see . . . thank you.' The secretary put the phone down and nodded to the chairman. But the interview was not quite over. A local member of the committee spoke up. 'Don't you have a piano?' 'No.' Bert was surprised at this. 'You know you have to declare valuables . . . We can't give you any money if you have valuables?' 'Yes, sir.' 'Now you're a musical family and I understand you have a piano.' 'No, sir, you've been misinformed. I've no piano.' Silence. 'Very well, Haley,' said the chairman, 'that will be all.' Bert went out rubbing his forehead.

They had to sign on for the dole every Monday, Wednesday and Friday, but they got paid on the Friday. From month to month the queues grew longer, until, when Bert arrived at half past eight, he found men standing four deep for a mile up the town. It took him till dinner time before he could sign on.

All kinds of folk, with all sorts of skills, stood silently beside him, in front or behind, shuffling slowly along. To Bert it was a miserable time. His looks wandered dully from the stained walls that shut him in, to the damp setts at his feet, slick with dirt. He could contemplate the itching yellow boil on the bristling neck in front of him, for slow pace after slow pace as the long morning dragged on. There was nothing else to do. Most of the men didn't even want to talk. One day he heard two ex-soldiers, though, thinking about what they had come to, and the words stuck in his memory. 'Dos't recall all them posters in Cleckheaton – "your country needs you" . . . and all that? . . .' The short one, still in khaki greatcoat, was saying. 'Well, me and me mate signed up and went . . . He had his head blown off, right at side of me . . . I wish it'd been mine.' Bert looked down the long, drab misery of the queue as he thought of this. At least it wasn't raining.

Valley of the Lost Souls

There was no hope to be found. When Bert had collected his dole money, and seen the groups of men hanging about street corners, leaning against grimy walls, or squatting on their haunches by the kerb, he went home miserable. Life wasn't easy on eighteen shillings a week, with mother getting older and less capable and the rent to pay and food to find for both of them. Bert couldn't bear hanging around with nothing to do. But there was nothing at all to do in Cleckheaton. So he got out.

When he was in the scouts Bert had really taken to life in camp, though they only went once or twice. It had been a great adventure, a long escape into the outer world. Now he thought nostalgically of a wood he had once visited, not far off the road to Halifax, near Shelf, a strange, secret wooded valley, hidden away in folds of ground that lay between the industrial towns like mother of pearl in the crusty corners of an old shell. The valley seemed to be calling Bert to leave the streets for a home with the feel of wild country about it.

He planned to sleep there just as a night's holiday with one friend. Everything was arranged, the blankets, billy-can and sandwiches wrapped in greaseproof paper, but then the timid friend let him down. Not to be disheartened Bert walked on alone towards adventure, and reached the valley in moonlight. Dark, rustling and mysterious as it was, he made himself creep the full length of it on tiptoe until he was sure that nothing unknown could surprise him. When he came to the beck that ran down the centre of the valley he stopped, catching a glimpse of movement out of the corner of his eye. What could it be? Bert watched, breathless, ready to run, and saw . . . a water rat. So he breathed again, but quietly, not to disturb it. The rat perched on a stump for a moment then dived into the water, emerged downstream, shook itself, silvery in the moonlight, went back to the stump and dived in again. Bert laughed to himself for the pleasure of it all, for a world where water rats dived in fun. What was there to be afraid of here? He had left fear behind him.

He walked on, catching the distant echo of a strange rasping noise in the meadow beyond the wood. It was a bird of some kind, surely. Then he saw it in the clear moonlight, running, long-necked, through the grass, like a cyclist behind a wall, its legs invisible. Two such laughs, and Bert was at home. He spread his blankets beside the stream and slept the sleep of the employed.

When he returned, to fret at home all day, finding it hard to sleep, Bert's thoughts turned to that secret valley. He had ten pounds saved. It would soon go, frittered away on the bits they needed and on small pleasures to relieve the boredom, fish and chips or a visit to the cinema. Now, if he bought a tent with the money, and lived out as a hermit, his room would be empty, and Mother could let it. That would be money coming into the house. Best of all, Bert would be away from the miseries of Cleckheaton, except when he went to sign on, or vainly to look for work. His Mother knew by now that it was no good objecting to Bert's ideas. So he went to see the farmer at Bob Den Farm. Aye, he remembered Bert. No, he didn't mind Bert camping. He could stay there as long as he liked if he gave a hand with the odd jobs now and then. Something about Bert's open-hearted enthusiasm made it difficult to say no.

It was a beautiful tent, white, with a flysheet made of Irish linen, high enough for Bert to stand up at the ridge, and absolutely waterproof. So Bert went into business as a hermit at once. He built a fireplace in the banking, sheltered by an overhanging tree from all but the heaviest rains. Thinking it over carefully, for he had the time, Bert devised a pair of sliding stones at either side, so that he only had to move them along to shelter the blaze from the wind, and could vary the size of the grate to match the pan or kettle he was using. It proved very effective. The farmer let him lift potatoes, carrots and turnips in return for help.

He had water to hand for drinking and washing. Bert slept on the ground, wrapped in his blankets, without a care in the world.

Winter came, and he had no intention of giving up his free life. He kept an eye on Mother when he had to go into Cleckheaton. One evening, about half past eight, he was walking back to camp through a small village when he saw the lights on in the butcher's shop, and the butcher himself, in straw-hat and striped apron, leaning against the door post, waiting to sell-off his remaining stock and close. Bert was wearing khaki shorts and shirt, no stockings, and old pumps with holes in them, so that his big toe stuck out. He always looked a skinny fellow with long naked shins, and something of a lantern jaw to complete the skeleton.

The butcher watched him coming along the road, and then, perhaps because he was a properly-fleshed advertisement for his own trade, he shouted across to Bert. 'Nah then, lad, hast' owt to eat?' Bert shook his head. 'Come over!' Bert went over. The butcher had him inside the shop, looked at him again, then took a good, hearty handful of stewing beef, it must have been over a pound weight, and wrapped it up in newspaper. 'Eat that, lad.' Bert looked at it. 'Why, thanks.' He didn't know what else to say, but the butcher didn't seem to mind, he simply laid a meaty hand on Bert's shoulder, though carefully, as if Bert might crumble under it, and propelled him on his way.

Bert found himself marching up the road with a soggy parcel in his hand, and rather puzzled by the whole affair. But that night he made an enormous stew, with the meat, and a panful of lifted carrots and potatoes. He stuffed himself till he could eat no more, then lay back beside the glowing ashes of his fire and watched the farm dog clean out the pan. That was bliss, and he told his stomach not to expect it every day. But the good butcher called him over every now and again throughout all the years he was a hermit and always with the look of a man who couldn't abide a living skeleton.

Word spread of this strange, half-naked hermit who lived in Sun Wood. It wasn't normal. Ordinary folk didn't hide from their fellows like that, and he obviously needed to be investigated. So the village policeman stopped him one day. 'Now then, lad, what are t'doing in yonder wood? Are t'T.B., or what?' 'No.' 'No . . . tha doesn't look it.' The policeman eyed an obviously healthy, if thin, Bert with increased suspicion. 'What's th'idea of camping in a wood . . . like that . . . by thisen? What's the game?' 'It's no game at all . . . I love it!' 'Well, tha must be daft, then.' But the policeman let him go.

It wasn't only officials who were incredulous. Even Bert's mates found the whole thing hard to stomach. He had one acquaintance who was a stoker at a mill, a married man who met Bert at a pub in Cleckheaton and wouldn't believe it. After he'd taken his half dozen pints, for he was a thirsty man on account of his calling, he told Bert why. 'Th' always told a good yarn, Bert. Th'art yarnin again.' Bert grinned. 'Nay, I'm not.' 'Th'art pullin my leg. I tell thee . . . It's nobbut a tale.' 'Right,' said Bert, 'I'll show thee . . . Meet me at t'river bridge, I'll tell thee where in a minute . . . after dinner on Sunday, say two o'clock, and I'll show thee. Bring t'wife wi' thee and I'll make tea.' 'Right, yer on!' 'I mean it,' said Bert. 'I'll be there,' said his mate, 'See thee Sunday.' Each of them winked in declaration that he wasn't taken in by the other. They drank up and parted.

Bert laid his preparations carefully, knowing his friend's weakness for ale, he went out and bought a dozen pint bottles. He went upstream from his camp, as far as the waterfall, hiding pairs of bottles at intervals in the water. He secreted a couple of glasses in his old army haversack. Then he went down to the bridge and hid under the arch, waiting for them to come.

The wife was audible from some distance away. 'He's noan here . . . I tell thee . . . gurt thick-head. He's noan here . . . Th'art lost. Don't know where th'are?' They came to the bridge and sat for a moment on the parapet. Bert could hear her sighing with manifest disgust. He waited a little longer, he could hear his friend scuffing his clogs in the dust, and the woman sighing regularly. Then he popped his head over the wall beside them. 'Sitha!' They jumped. 'Here I am!' She looked daggers at him, having no sense of humour at all. But eventually he managed to persuade her not to walk off in a huff, and to come into the wood, tempted by the thought of tea. They had to admit that the camp was really there, and even that you could make a good brew with the beck water. After tea, Bert asked if they'd like a walk in the woods and a look at the waterfall. She was sitting comfortably on his blankets by then, digesting a couple of slices of cake, so she said, 'I'll stop here. You two go for a walk.'

They climbed up the hillside, between the trees. It was hot, and his friend was sweating, so Bert stopped for a moment to give him a breather. He looked around, slowly, panting. 'By gum, it's all right, is this, Bert . . . I didn't believe thee . . . but it's grand.' 'Aye,' Bert replied, choosing his words carefully, 'what could you wish for better'n this?' His mate thought for a moment. 'Nowt,' he said, 'but I'd be a bit fast for a pub . . . it's too far off.' 'Dost fancy a drink?' 'What's t'talking about? . . . Th'art always on wi' tales?' 'Dost want a pint o' beer?' 'Aye!' He spoke with the feeling of a man whose tenderest hopes were under attack. 'Well, just sit thee there.' And Bert galloped off down to the stream, to return with two dripping, cool bottles. He opened them, then produced the glasses from his haversack. His mate, whose complete astonishment kept him gasping like an overheated fish, took the beer as if it were jewels suddenly produced from Aladdin's cave and lowered it reverently down his steaming throat.

When it had gone, he sighed, eyed the empty glass and said, in his usual, lyrical way, 'I've never had a pint like that in my bloody life.' 'Could tha do with another?' He nodded, too impressed to speak. Bert vanished towards the stream again. They walked on after a while, in a leisurely fashion, and finished all dozen bottles between them. The walk must have taken longer than expected, because his wife was up and about, pacing round the campsite like a reproachful dog expecting its dinner. One look was enough. 'I know where you lot've been.' They looked at her. 'To t'pub!' 'No, we haven't!' 'You're lying!' 'I'm not,' Bert replied, sounding as indignant as he could without letting laughter creep into his voice. 'Where have you been then?' 'We've just been up t'wood!' 'I don't believe a word you say . . . and I never shall do, neither. You can talk all day . . . but I know you've been in a pub.' With that she grabbed her husband's arm and marched him unsteadily off to the road.

Bert was still chuckling to himself as he sat beside the fire that beautiful, clear night and smoked his cherry-wood pipe. He didn't feel lonely at all, in fact, there were times when he counted it a blessing that he was an only son, single and without kids. What would he have done in such hard times if he were tied like that? The sky was clear and cooling rapidly. He wrapped a blanket round himself, looked at the shafts of red-light spreading from the fire, and listened in peace to the trickle of the waterfall. At such a time he'd have liked to know how to write music. Bert looked up at the constellations, wheeling above his head, just beyond the treetops. 'Why me?' he thought. 'Why can't my mates live like this?' It was beautiful, solemn, alone in his valley. Then he couldn't help chuckling over the day's events. 'They think I'm crackers.' He lay back and puffed at his pipe.

Not that the world could bear to leave him alone in such disgraceful idleness. The parson stopped to talk to him, seriously, one day as he sat by the water-wheel outside the old mill, waiting for the pub to open. The parson was a fine, tall, strapping man, well-educated, a Cambridge blue in his day. 'Now then, are you the young man that lives in that wood, all alone?' 'Yes.' 'Why? I can't understand it . . . Do you go to Church?' 'No.' 'Why not, son?' 'I've no interest in it.' 'Why not come up to our old church. It's a lovely place . . . you'll like it, and I'd like to see you there.' 'Well,' Bert answered defensively, for he was getting tired of this cross-examination after all the others, 'I've nowt to dress up in.' 'It doesn't matter . . . so long as you come in a clean cricket shirt, or something similar, you'll be all right.' Then he asked Bert. 'What was your religion?' 'Church of England,' was the answer, as Bert thought of all the times he'd sat beside his mother and father at church in Cleckheaton.

Bert resolved to move to the attack. 'I suppose you had a good education?' The parson sounded surprised. 'Yes,' he said, 'I went to Cambridge.' 'I suppose you know all that Latin stuff, and Greek philosophy and all that?' . . . The parson nodded. 'Now, I've been seeking a philosophy . . . and I think I've found it here.' He pointed towards his wood. The parson made as if to speak, for he wasn't used to being at the receiving end of a sermon, but Bert was too quick for him. 'How can you talk to me? Say I came up to your church . . . morning or evening, it doesn't matter. If it's morning I can repeat your morning service by heart from beginning to end. The only thing I can't repeat is your sermon. So, what are you going to talk to me about? How can you get down to my level, as a man who's out of work and nobody wants him? He goes out seeking work, and what do they do? They shut t'door in his face. Can you give me a philosophy from your Greeks to tell me how to face this life?

'Do you know how I face it? When I get around my campfire at night, smoking my pipe like an Indian? It might be a beautiful, starry night . . . it's so clear you can see right behind 'em. They aren't on a backcloth, they're hung. I look up at them . . . and the silence . . . sat by the fire. It's wonderful. There's something above man, and I'm satisfied . . . You can't satisfy me like that through your sermons.'

The parson had the decency to go away without trying to give Bert an answer. Maybe that was why Bert felt some slight pangs of guilt that he'd rejected a well-intentioned offer. He mulled it over, and decided, a week or two later, that he would go to church. Dressed as best he could, in white cricket shirt as clean as he could manage, Bert popped in through the door and sat at the back, in as much decent obscurity as he could find. But they all stared at him, all those people dressed for their Sunday dinners, gold watch chains and all. When the service began, his friend the parson wasn't taking it, and to cap it all, the organ wasn't playing, only a harmonium. A service without music, and all that cold steam of disapproval rising round him, it proved too much for Bert. He slipped out again.

He waited outside the pub, which was just across from the church, and went in as soon as it opened. A fair number of men were on the same business, and an old man collared him as he got his drink. 'Hast'a been to t'kirk, lad?' 'I have that.' 'What were it like?' 'Well, it were a bit dull.' The old man laughed maliciously. 'No organist, were there?' 'No.' 'No . . . dost' know why?' 'No, I don't.' 'Well, I'll tell thee . . . I'm t'man as pumps t'organ . . . and I'm on strike.' Bert waited to hear the rest of the tale. He was obviously going to get it whether he wanted it or not. 'That new organist! He wants to alter all t'services . . . I've been here thirty year, and I'm noan going to pump no wind into yon organ just to play them new tunes of his . . . I'm on strike . . . and I reckon I've done right.' He waited for Bert to react. 'Well, it were a bit miserable in there.' 'Aye, I thought so.' The old man looked pleased with this satisfactory news. 'Well, I'd best be going.' And that was the end of Bert's church-going.

They began to call it the valley of the lost souls, Bert's kingdom, but he didn't care. He went naked in summer, patrolling with skinny legs, his beak of a nose sniffing all the winds, learning to move noiselessly and watch the wild things. All kinds of odd folk came to this solitude from time to time. Once, at midnight, he came on two well-dressed men sitting on a tree stump whispering to each other about shares and profits.

On another occasion he woke during the night with a sense of danger, looked out, for he always kept the flaps open, and grasped his mallet. Someone was crawling towards him on hands and knees. 'Let me in,' he bleated, 'let me sleep here.' 'Get off,' Bert answered fiercely, 'clear off or I'll get thee!' The man turned and fled at the sight of

Bert's upraised mallet, and vanished, blundering through the bushes. Bert listened till he was gone. He wouldn't have that fellow in his tent. He was a notorious hogger, a peeping-tom who crept about in darkness to watch the country couples at their pleasures. His wife must have locked the door on him again. Bert felt no pity for the miserable creature. He simply went to sleep again, holding his mallet.

Another day he was on naked patrol when he caught sight of someone at the top of the valley. He was obviously a lad from the local grammar school, out in his uniform, cap, blazer and all. Bert moved after this solitary explorer to see what he was up to, when, suddenly, the lad slipped, fell, and rolled down the hillside. He landed only a couple of feet from where Bert was standing, hidden behind a bush. The lad got up and brushed himself down, obviously shaken a little and muttering to himself. Bert waited. He hadn't been seen, that he knew. Then, when the lad had pulled himself together again, he reached out, touched his shoulder and said in his most cultured voice, 'Do you know, you're trespassing!' Flat on his back the lad went a second time! Then he was off, running through the trees to escape from the strange apparition that had materialized beside him. No wonder they called it the valley of the lost souls.

Mind you, Bert wasn't there all the time. Occasionally he got some temporary job. Once he fixed up a trip to France, to see the battlefields where his heroes had died, to visit the graves and lay flowers on behalf of those who were left behind, the widows, mothers and sisters of the dead. He came back with a French beret to wear beside his fire, and the memory of the endless rows of white crosses, the tortured earth grown green again, and the fields of poppies. Something more to think about, quietly, slowly, as he chewed at his philosophy under the stars.

Seven years passed by. It was 1934, and Bert was thirty-one. Times and ideas were changing, and the war, slump, general strike and all, seemed long ago, part of history. Bert landed a regular job, minding an engine, and moved on from that to better work. It paid well enough, once he could face the monotonous hours and the imprisonment between four walls. They kept him busy, tied to work. Then he met a girl at the mill, a lass called Annie May.

One day, as he stood, looking up at the sky after working through to the middle of Saturday afternoon, Bert thought to himself, 'I'm chained as it is . . . I might as well do the job properly.' So he proposed to Annie May, surrendered his freedoms, and accepted the ordinariness of life. He married, bought a house, had two daughters, and found a good job in engineering. What could be a happier ending?

Jennie Porter

and the Barges

All the principal rivers of Yorkshire flow into the Humber, and in the past they carried the County's trade with them. Hull squatted on the north bank of the Humber estuary in a flat, fen landscape, low lying and marshy, that stretched to the east coast, drawing cargoes to it, growing into a mighty port. Those large sailing barges, the Humber keels, could sail upriver from Hull as far as York, or take the canal to Leeds, Wakefield and Sheffield. Sturdy vessels that linked the County together in a network of trade, like arterial blood spreading into the outstretched hand.

Jenny Porter was born in 1892, a native of Beverley, the delightful old market town set on the edge of the Yorkshire Wolds some ten miles north of Hull. Beverley beck linked the town to the River Hull, making it a centre of trade and boatbuilding, a home for many families who worked the Humber keels. Jenny spent most of her young life on her father's keel, returning to Beverley for the occasional schooling. She stayed afloat most of her life, 'though she was always frightened of water', and learnt to cook a sea-pie that would win any keelman's heart.

Jennie of Beverley

'I think we'll have a fire in t'cabin today,' said Mother, 'I reckon paint'll be set.' They were waiting at Park Hill colliery to take a load of coal for the return trip to Hull, and Dad had taken the opportunity of re-painting the cabin, after Mother had suggested it once or twice. So they laid out beds in the hold. Fortunately, the up-river cargo had been wheat, and it wasn't so mucky as coal or cement. But still they began to feel the need of a proper wash after a week or so. The linseed-oil smell of painting was a background to everything they ate, and it took a deal of a time to dry. Mother wasn't going to wait any longer. She didn't like waiting, or being crossed in her arrangements, even by new paintwork. Though, mind you, she'd had a difficult life.

'I'll go and light t'fire,' she said to Jennie, 'then I'll have a real good wash.' Dad and Bob were on the stay talking to some colliers. 'Go and get me a bowl o' water,' she said to Jennie. Now Jennie couldn't have been more than six or seven at the time, because it was two or three years later that her brother David drowned in Alexandra Dock at Hull, and that was in May 1900. But she was used to working on the keel, so she lowered a bucket over the side, let it fill in the canal, and then struggled to haul it back up to fill the big, tin washbowl for her mother. It was all she could do to carry the bowl, two-handed, across the deck to the cabin hatchway.

The cabins, fore and aft, were both below decks in a keel, with the cargo hold between them. To get to the main cabin, which was aft, you climbed into a sort of raised box on the deck, which could be shut at night, or in foul weather, with a rolling cover, moving in grooves, like the lid of an old-fashioned desk. A ladder went down into the cabin, and under the ladder was the coal-locker, conveniently placed so that it could be filled from the hold. Mother had to move the ladder out of the way so that she could get at the coal to light the fire.

Jennie staggered over to the hatch with her bowl of canal water. It was dark in the cabin, but she could hear her mother moving. So she lowered the bowl as far as her child's arms could reach. 'Have you got hold, Mother?' Silence. She called again. 'Mother?' Some indistinct words filtered up from below, and she felt a little of the weight taken off the bowl, so she let go, glad to ease her aching hands.

Too soon! The bowl tipped, swivelled against the corner of the ladder, where it had been lodged, and fell, full on top of Mother, who was still bent over, mining deep in the coal locker. The drop was about seven feet from hatch to cabin floor. The noise was amazing in that confined space.

Mother emerged from the hatchway, dripping wet, her face like a fury. Jennie fled along the deck, screaming. Mother came after her seeking a rope-end. Dad hurried over. 'Whatever's the matter?' 'I'll kill her. Look what she's done. I'll kill her when I get hold of her!' Jennie ran to Dad, clung to the strong wool of his guernsey, feeling the rope-patterns hard in her hands. Dad was kind, never had a harsh word for her. But Mother grabbed her and led her away, pushed her down the ladder, and went to find a bit of line-end. She really laid it on.

Jennie remembered to be careful after that, because she couldn't lie on her back for a week. Her skin was not just bruised, but bleeding in ragged lines from the coarse rope. Dad was as angry as he dared be. 'If there was a policeman hereabouts I'd have thee transported for what tha's done to that lass!' he said to Mother once or twice as poor Jennie hobbled painfully about the vessel in the morning, the fresh scabs catching on her vest. Mother looked sullen, that was all. Jennie knew that working keels was a rough life, and she always had good-healing flesh.

Her earliest memories were of life on board. Carried into the cabin in a basket soon after she was born, in Beverley, close by the beck, she slept to the rocking motion of the keel, and saw the hanging brass oil-lamp sway, far out of reach, below the deck-planking. Jennie grew up, quite naturally, in this moving world. The keel was home, a keel called *Jennie of Beverley*, and whether she was named after the boat, or the boat after her, was hard to tell. As far as importance went, it must have been the boat that had priority, for Jennie was last, youngest member of a family of twelve children. The 'whipper-in' they called her, only child of her father and mother both.

Nearly all the family worked on the keels, one way or another. It was traditional in the parts around Hull, and much of the heavy traffic in wheat, coal, iron, slag, broken stone, palm-nuts, wood-pulp, even epsom salts and treacle, was carried in the broad, square-rigged keelboats, that could sail up the wide, turbulent Humber, with its shifting channels, and also travel far inland to the industrial towns of West Yorkshire. They were not barges, certainly not, but proper sailing vessels, with a long history of building that could be traced back to the trading-ships of the vikings.

Solid, broad vessels were the keels, with a forty foot mast and square sail of unbleached cotton that gave them the look of a ship out of history. *Jennie of Beverley* was made of pine boards two inches thick, on an oak keel. She was carvel-built, the joints plugged with oak, and her hull then well-protected with a coating of tar. You could lie still at night and hear the creaking of her timbers when the swell came up the Humber.

Both Jennies came from Beverley, a charming old market town that sits on a spur of the Yorkshire Wolds, low, rolling hills dividing the flat Vale of York from the even flatter coastlands of Holderness. In those days, when inland navigation still served the towns and countryside with a fleet of silent, slow-moving, but weight-carrying vessels, virtually every river that could be made to float traffic was in use, and where the rivers failed, canals were built. There were shipyards in Beverley itself, not far from the crocketed twin towers of its magnificent thirteenth century minster, and Beverley beck, with its wharves, oil-cake mill and coal heaps gave direct navigation to the river Hull. Downstream lay the great port of Kingston-upon-Hull, with all its thriving businesses, a mighty fleet of deep-water trawlers, and the export and import trade of much of Yorkshire.

Almost every river in the County flows into the Humber, and even with larger vessels, such as *Jennie*, it was possible to go up the Ouse as far as York, to take the Aire and Calder canal to Leeds, to follow the Don past Doncaster to Sheffield, or to take the river Trent half-way to Lincoln. They even sailed down the coast to take coal to Grimsby on one memorable occasion, though keels were not built for seafaring (when fully laden they had only a few inches of freeboard, and waves could wash right over the decks, even in good weather).

Jennie grew up in this travelling world, watching half Yorkshire pass her by. Sometimes they took a tug up river, and then hoisted sail to follow the Ouse as far as Selby, with its white-stone Abbey that reminded her of the Minster at home. Then they passed through flat, arable land, collecting a ton or two of grain in sacks from farmers at jetties or landing-places near the agricultural villages. The land was often hidden by high embankments, depending on the water, flood tide or ebb, and the height of the river. They would seek land-marks to steer by, even when the banks were under water, high church spires, such as Hemingbrough, a few miles from Selby. Its point was always visible by day, and the local children waved to them as they passed.

As they came nearer the end of the day, Jennie would say to her Dad, 'Can I go and sit i' t'boat?' They always towed a little coggy-boat behind, and she learnt to row it by sculling behind with a single oar. 'Aye.' 'Can I take a bit o' bread and milk?' 'Ask thy mother.' And if Mother was feeling kindly, not huddling her shawl tightly round her shoulders, huffing at the world, then Jennie might be given a scrape of condensed milk on a piece of bread, climb into the boat and be alone. It was a real delight, to drift along like that, and watch the world go by, licking the sweetness off the bread.

Dad and Mother were old, far too old to play with, and too busy. In the evenings, though, she might sit in the cabin, while the wind blew across the hatch-cover and rattled the aft-rollers above them, and play Ludo with her Dad. Mother didn't really approve of games, and she said playing-cards 'had the devil in 'em', wouldn't have them in the boat. So Mother would sew, or do the ironing on the top of the transom locker with a flat-iron heated on the stove. She couldn't read or write, but she could reckon to a ha'penny. That was just like Mother, practical in all her ways. They didn't have much room, and Dad had to tuck his chair right against the table-flap to leave Mother space to turn, whilst Jennie was crammed into the corner of the bedside locker.

But it was very cosy in the cabin, when the wind was up. Coal glowed, flaring intermittently in the small enclosed grate with its elaborate, black, iron surround of cast fruit and flowers. Mirrors at the back of the buffet, the best cupboard above the transom locker, with its brass handles, turned half-columns in red mahogany and the pride of mother's china inside, reflected back some of the glow. Dad would light his churchwarden pipe and draw in the cool smoke with relaxed enjoyment. At Christmas he allowed himself a cigar. If it was cold, and Bob had no fire in the forecastle, where he slept, and where the oven was, then he would crowd in as well, and it got quite tight. Dad would cock his head at the wind when they weren't at proper moorings, and say 'Hast' got t'mud-hook well out?' Bob would look at him. He was a reliable mate. 'What dost' reckon, Dad?' 'Aye, all right then,' and they'd get out the dominoes.

When it was bedtime they packed Jennie into her tiny bunk just aft of the coal locker. Bob went out of the hatch and across the deck to the fo'c's'le. Then Mother dimmed the lamp and she and Dad got into bed. They had a lovely big bunk, mahogany panelled, with sliding doors to shut off the cabin. It was all of four feet wide at the head end, tapering a bit as it went aft. They had a feather mattress and pillows, really snug.

Dad would always put out the light and get in last. He could lie, sound asleep, and know by feel that the keel was safe, no proper change of wind or tide disturbed him. Even when they were moored on the Trent and a tidal bore rocked the boat like a bucking horse, Dad knew in his sleep that it was no danger. Local folk called that 'the Ager', and it was an awesome sight to watch, roaring up river towards them, six feet high. But Jennie slept sound, confident of her Dad's experience. In the mornings, though, she might wake, cold, to see icicles hanging from the deck-lights, and shiver at the thought of going out on deck.

In summer and fine weather keeling could be a grand life. Once, they were moored at Stanley Ferry and Mother and Dad decided to go into Wakefield to shop. 'I want to go too,' said Jennie. 'You stop wi' Bob and you'll be all right.' 'I want to go.' Bob took her hand. 'You stop wi' me, Gin, and I'll buy thee a tin o' milk.' Jennie loved condensed milk more than shopping, so she nodded and waited on board as Bob went round the corner for her present. He came back with a big tin, twice the normal size. 'Here th'are, Gin.' Bob opened it with his pocket-knife. 'Now just sit quiet and sup that . . . but mind you leave some for me.' He went off to clear out the fo'c's'le. Well, Jennie sucked at the tin, and shook it, sucked it again, waited a bit for Bob, and sucked some more. Bob was a long time in the fo'c's'le, but at last he came out to collect his share. 'You greedy little bitch! You've never left me a bit!' He shook the can and then shook his fist at Jennie. 'You'll be taken badly . . . and serve you right!' But Jennie was fond of Bob, so it didn't matter for long.

In those days they always kept a dog on board, in its kennel on deck beside the waterkeg. She was called Nell, a little, white, smooth-haired bitch, with big, splayed-out paws and a small patch of tan on her nose. Jennie loved Nell and needed her as a playmate. Of course, the dog got away when she could, and met other dogs at the wrong time, as animals will. Mother shook her head at the prospect, and muttered about 'getting rid of her', but with her own family of twelve she hadn't much right to complain.

Nell had her pups on board, five of them. Four were white like Nell, and the fifth pure black except for a brown mark on the nose like his mother's. Jennie had a fine time playing with the pups, sometimes she even dared to sneak one down into the cabin. But they couldn't be kept, and one by one Mother found homes for them, until only the black one was left, and he was promised.

They were taking a cargo of wood pulp to a wallpaper factory in Barnsley when Nell vanished. Jennie and Mother called for her, looked everywhere, but she never returned. Jennie was upset. She cried at the loss, but Dad told her they would keep the last pup themselves. 'What'll we call him, love?' He was growing fast, had bigger paws than his mother. 'Heaven knows what his dad was.' 'Should call him "Tiny",' said Bob, 'he'll be a fair size.' Just like a lad to say that, but the name stuck. Jennie took to Tiny, and encouraged him to grow with a share of her bread and milk and the licking-out of her mug of tea. 'Don't spoil yon dog,' said Mother when she caught her at it. But it did no good.

Tiny grew up to be a faithful old soul, though he still loved his dish of milk. In winter time he would sit in his kennel close beside Dad when Dad was at the tiller. One cold morning they had a cargo to take upriver from Hull to Beverley and Driffield, and Dad said to Mother, 'I'll have that drop o'rum, my lass.' He generally took a drop of rum and milk on such occasions, to warm himself up. He was busy at that time, winding the sheet in. It was a long haul to Beverley beck if you got a head-wind rack.

'I'll have that drop o'rum, now, lass.' Mother looked up the cabin hatchway. 'Where's that drop o'rum, lass?' 'It's there!' 'It isn't.' 'Well, I gave it thee!' Mother came up the ladder and pointed at a mug on the deck by Dad's feet. 'There's no rum in it.' They both looked at Tiny, who was licking his chops in a guilty fashion behind the kennel.

'Blessed dog's supped it,' said Dad. 'I'll kill thee,' said Mother advancing on Tiny with her buttoned boots, prepared to catch him a hard kick in the ribs. Tiny knew about this, he'd come across it before, and so he slunk up to the fore-end and from there he hopped onto the bank. Mother gave up the pursuit and returned to the cabin. Dad lit his pipe up once they were under way. He generally laid out twelvepence halfpenny on a quarter pound of tobacco in Hull and it lasted out the slow trip to Driffield that took most of a week.

'Where's our Tiny?' Jennie asked her Dad. 'Nay, I don't know, happen he's gone to that fish shop in Little Dock Street. Tha knows he'll sit there and wait for bits.' Well, Jennie thought no more of it until late in the day, when Tiny still hadn't appeared and they had followed the river right through Hull and out into the countryside. 'Tiny's not here, Dad!' 'Nay, poor little beggar must have got lost.' They were all a bit quiet at this, but they couldn't stop and go looking for him. They had cargoes to deliver.

The journey took a week, and Tiny didn't find them. They reached home and settled in for a brief rest on land. 'Well, we've heard the last of Tiny,' said Dad. But one evening they had eaten dinner, and Dad was sat with his pipe, when suddenly he jerked up, clenched his fingers, and snapped the stem in two. 'There's our Tiny!' he said, at the sound of a scratching at the door.

The poor dog came limping in, thin, exhausted, his feet rubbed raw and a shotgun pellet in his backside, but home again. Wasn't Jennie delighted to see the faithful old soul, to get him some dinner and rub him down, and finally to make him comfortable by the fire. 'Dad'll need a new pipe,' Mother said, with no comment on the waste involved, which was warm words for her. Jennie made a special trip to the old clay-pipe maker in his alley workshop up the town to get a new churchwarden for her Dad.

Jennie went to the Minster School when they were in Beverley, where she learnt to be a good reader and write a fair hand. Sometimes the kiddie-catcher would be waiting at Beverley lock when they came upriver. 'School tomorrow, Jennie!' Then she knew she had to go. But her real learning was day by day on the keel, for that was the way to make a living. Formal schooling just didn't fit the youngest daughter of a keeling family, used to her freedom, to certain work for her Mother, but also to pleasant little bits of spoiling from her Dad and older brothers.

Jennie simply couldn't take all the regularities of school seriously. There was Miss, one day, up on the desk, marching, on the spot, and singing a patriotic song to them, for it was the time of the second Boer War. Jennie sat right in front of her. Miss began to get into the swing of her demonstration. She lifted up her skirts, stepping out, and Jennie watched with interest as the folds rose ever higher, until there peeped out the frills of Miss's long knickers, the lace frothing around the edges. Jennie couldn't help it, she cracked out laughing at the sight of such a soldierly figure.

The whole class followed suit. Miss stopped marching, insulted, wounded deeply in her personal and patriotic pride. 'Jane Porter! Come out here.' She looked in her desk, found nothing, and took a ha'penny from her purse. 'Take this! Go to St Andrews Street. Buy a halfpenny cane and bring it back here!' Jennie fled through the busy streets of Beverley, came back and was beaten, soundly, across both hands. My, did it sting.

'I'm not going to that school any more, Mother.' 'What for?' 'She hit me, and I was only laughing.' 'Did she now!' Mother might be hard, but she would stand by her family. So they took Jennie away and paid, somehow, for her to go to Miss Ross's in Walkergate, where she learnt lady-like accomplishments, such as knitting and sewing. She was the whipper-in, so they wouldn't have any more children to pay for.

Mother took full advantage of her daughter's painfully acquired culture. 'Come on. Get that book out! Do a bit o'reading!' She would say on long winter evenings in the cabin, and Jennie had to borrow a stock of paper-bound books about Polly Green and Coulsha the black servant-girl, to entertain her mother. It was the very stuff of romance.

Both sides of her education had continued in this way

for a little while, until the disasters of the year 1900 brought changes in the family. They had been very close in that small, double-fronted house, being a family of twelve, even though most times some were scattered over Yorkshire in keels, or farmed out with relatives. Jennie still doesn't know how they all fitted in.

David was twenty-two when he drowned in Alexandra Dock, and George nineteen when he followed suit within the year. Bob had work on offer, and he left the *Jennie of Beverley*. So Dad turned to his youngest daughter. Her education was almost complete. 'Fo'c's'le's empty, Jennie. There's room for thee.' 'Aye, Dad.' 'Tha' can be mate. I'll learn thee.' 'Aye, Dad.' 'Right, lass, it's down to Hull tomorrow. Start off at five in the morning!'

The Colonel's Servant

Jennie was having a holiday in August 1907. She was fifteen years old, wiry, slim, with long hair that hung down to her waist when she combed it out, a self-reliant, independent girl, well-suited to be mate of a keel. Dad was moored in Queen's dock, Hull, doing bits and pieces of work, not expecting to sail for a week or two, so Jennie had gone to stay with a married half-sister in Beverley with the idea of joining the keelmen's aquatic sports. She might just have a chance at the sculling race, being quite at home in a coggy-boat.

The day before the sports she was at her sister's house in Minster Moorgate when there was a knock at the door, and a brisk, middle-aged lady came in. 'I'm from St Mary's Manor,' she said, 'Colonel Duncombe's house. I'm looking for a young girl for a temporary place in the house. We're short of a kitchen maid.' She explained to Jennie's sister why she had called. Meanwhile Jennie was thinking 'Why not,' she liked a bit of a change, wanted to see other sides of life, and she knew Dad could manage for a month, which was what the housekeeper proposed. The verbal hunt for suitable candidates was running slow, when Jennie suddenly asked, 'Will I do?'

Her sister looked at her in sharp surprise. The house-keeper said, 'Well, have you been in service before?' 'Yes,' said Jennie, explaining that when Bob had first married and moved into the fo'c's'le with his bride, she had worked as kitchen-maid for Mrs Green, of the printing family, for nearly half a year. 'I'll have to see what the Colonel says,' was the lady's only comment, but she seemed pleased to have found someone. Jennie did rather wonder about her rash suggestion when the housekeeper was gone. 'Whatever's come over thee?' her sister asked, and Jennie didn't know what to say. She had just felt like helping out, and trying something different, meeting other folk, young men perhaps.

The lady was back later. 'Yes,' she confirmed, 'Colonel Duncombe would like to see you. I have your character from Mrs Green, and we think you'll suit.' 'Oh,' said Jennie. It all seemed cut and dried. 'When can you come?' 'Well, I'm here for the aquatic sports. I'll come after.' 'We'll see you first thing on Friday morning, then, and show you what to do.'

Jennie was in a proper pickle. She daren't tell Dad. He needed her as mate. She certainly wasn't going to tell Mother. It was dreadful to think what Mother would say. 'You, taking a place!' That was her sister's comment. 'My! Dad'll play up hangman when he gets to hear.' 'Well, it's only temporary, only for a month,' Jennie replied in explanation and consolation. She wasn't very keen herself, but she had given her word, and would go through with it.

St Mary's Manor wasn't so bad either. Jennie didn't have a great deal to do, because Colonel Duncombe's family were living in his brother's country house, Kilnwick Percy, near Pocklington on the road to York. So the Colonel himself had only to be served lunch in his study every day, and sometimes tea before he took the train back to Kilnwick in the evening.

When she had been working there for a fortnight the butler called her to the study at lunch time. 'The boss wants to see you.' 'What's he want to see me for?' 'You're to go to Kilnwick, they're a scullery-maid short.' 'I'm not going to Kilnwick, I don't know where it is!' 'It's near Pocklington, you'd best go along and see.'

The butler went back into the study and spoke to the Colonel. She could hear his brassy, military voice through the thickness of the door. He frightened her, with his pompous, critical ways, his staring red face, pop-eyes and waxed moustache. It was almost as if Colonel Duncombe played a part, as a younger son, and brother to a General. Forced to earn his living as a bank manager, he out-militarized an entire regiment, and dealt with his staff as if they were all mess-orderlies in the colonies.

Jennie was sent inside. She daren't look him in the face. 'I hear you don't want to go to Kilnwick!' 'No, sir . . . I don't know where it is . . . and I've never been to Pocklington.' 'Well, a girl at Kilnwick's left, and you'll have to help until I can get a new maid in York.' 'Well, sir, I didn't want this job.' Jennie was recovering a little of her keelman's independent spirit. 'What did you take it for?' 'I only came temporary.' 'Well, you're my servant, and you'll have to go!'

What could a fifteen year old from the working classes say in reply. She really didn't want to leave Beverley, and Dad would be expecting her back anytime. But next afternoon a cab came for her and her boxes, both of them. Colonel Duncombe arrived at the station, saw her waiting, said 'Follow me' and walked on. Jennie followed to the train, where he handed her a ticket and left her to get into a second class carriage, whilst he got into a first. The train hissed out of Beverley, and across the gentle hills of the Yorkshire Wolds towards Pocklington. Jennie, slightly worried, slightly annoyed with herself for being so soft, but not sure what else she could do, sat and thought, 'At least it's only temporary.'

They arrived at Pocklington station. The Colonel came over to her. 'Sit down there,' he said pointing to a seat with his cane, 'a conveyance will come for you.' She was not to travel to the big house in the same trap as her master. She waited for a while, then a porter came over. 'Are you for Kilnwick, miss?' 'Yes.' 'Oh, you'll be ages afore you get there. I wouldn't go to Kilnwick myself.' He shook his head and walked away. Jennie wondered what all the mystery was about. Everything was rather disturbing, as if she was being carried along by a current she couldn't resist. Where would it end?

It was a fine evening, but she still had to wait a while. At last a man in leggings came over to her. 'Are you for Kilnwick, miss?' 'Yes.' 'Come along, and I'll put your things in the trap.' Jennie sighed and obeyed. The road rose steeply from Pocklington, white in the late afternoon sun of that August day. It was pleasant, hilly countryside, but quite empty once they left the town, no village near the big house. Bearing left off the road, they came over a slight rise and saw a gateway in front of them. Behind it lay an expanse of parkland, and, in the distance a formal-looking, pedimented house, standing alone in the fields. It looked unfriendly. The groom pointed with his whip. 'That's Kilnwick,' he said.

They rolled on over the gravel of the driveway, and, as the house grew larger it seemed even less welcoming. Big, stone columns, rows of regular windows, like some particularly official town-hall. The trap turned a corner past the house. Perhaps it was better at the back. But the back was even worse, more like a barracks, built in yellowish brick, with scattered windows here and there in the high walls. No money had been wasted on the servants' quarters. The house was all front.

Jennie got down. She didn't like it, but she had to go in. It was about six o'clock, and all the servants were gathered in the kitchen, hot and smelling of fat – cook, housemaids, under-housemaids, kitchen maid, butler, footmen, ladies' maid. All turned to stare at the new scullery-maid, who felt as welcome as an old dishcloth. This was cook's province, and cook spoke first. 'Oh, we've been waiting. We wondered if you'd come.' 'I'm not stopping,' said

Jennie, right away. 'That's what you think.' 'Well I'm not. I've only come temporary.' They laughed. Jennie wanted to run off.

'Would you like a cup of tea . . . or would you rather change first?' They were all staring at her. 'I'll go change.' 'Maggie,' said cook to the under-housemaid, 'take Miss Porter up to her bedroom.' Maggie seemed a friendly enough girl. She began to giggle once they were safe from observation, and Jennie felt a little better. 'There you are,' she said, after they had wandered through endless waxy corridors and up scrubbed back-stairs. 'I'll leave you while you get changed.'

Jennie sat down, dazed, on a bed, and looked round. There were two beds, two of everything. 'At least I'll have a bed-mate,' she thought. She would need someone to talk to, to confide in, in this cold place. She stared at the other bed, then let her gaze drift for a while over the yellow-washed walls and the high, cold ceiling. Maggie peered in. 'Haven't you got changed yet?' 'I don't know what to change into.' 'Oh well, put your print on.' 'Print! At this time of night?' 'Oh yes! Work starts now.'

So Jennie put on her print dress and the apron and white cap she'd had at Beverley, and came downstairs. Fortunately most of the servants had left the kitchen, and cook said 'Do you want a cup of tea now?' 'Yes, please.' So she had tea and a jam sandwich. 'We'd best get started,' said cook, before she was really finished, 'can you fry chips?' 'Yes, I think so.'

A long range stretched down one wall of the kitchen, black lead and steel, with hot plates inset in the top. Cook put her to work chopping potatoes fine for game-chips. 'Shooting party for dinner tonight,' she said. 'Can you skin hares?' 'I've never seen one.' 'Well, you're scullery maid – you'll have to!'

Cook took her into the meat larder. A large, furry hare was hanging from a hook in the corner. Its pop-eyes had blurred over with a dull film, the blood on its fur was dry and caked. The smell made Jennie feel sick. Cook took it down and started skinning. 'I'll show you tonight – but I shan't do it after.' Like a surgeon in medical school, she began to show Jennie how to cut and peel back the skin. The flesh was almost green, very strong smelling. Jennie retched at the sight. 'It's mawky,' she said, 'I can't touch owt like that . . . It's bad.' 'It's been hung,' said cook, who didn't seem to mind. 'They have 'em while they're high, cooked in wine and herbs.' 'They'll want it an' all,' said Jennie as she marvelled at the revolting habits of the upper classes. She wouldn't eat meat like that herself.

Well, she finished the chips. Then she sliced kidney beans. The trays had to be got ready for the day and night nurses, who ate together in the nursery. Master Archie's own dinner was also sent up. He was quite unfit to eat at table with his parents, and often the plates came back smashed. 'Don't put out a knife for Master Archie,' cook warned, 'just spoon and fork.' 'Why, what's up with him?' 'You'll see!' Then it was time to serve up the servants' dinner through the hatch in the servants' hall.

Pots began to come in, piles and piles of pots, and Jennie started washing up. Ten o'clock, and the pots from the shooting party upstairs were still descending, towers of plates, trays of glasses, grease and bones. Jennie straightened her back at the sink and wiped her forehead with a soapy arm. The footman came in. 'Haven't you finished washing-up yet?' 'No, and I shan't finish it tonight by the look of them pots! I've never seen so many in my life!' The kitchen maid came in and offered to help, since it was Jennie's first night. 'But I shan't help another time. I've my own work to do.' Then the footman came back again. 'I'll have to turn your lights out, you know. It's after ten.' 'Well, what'll we do?' asked Jennie. 'Oh, you'll have to finish by candlelight.'

At eleven o'clock a weary scullery-maid climbed the back stairs at Kilnwick Percy, carrying a chicken leg and a portion of cold rice pudding now that she had time for her own supper. She was to start at six next morning by cleaning out the fireplace in the housekeeper's room and serving breakfast to that fine lady and the butler.

Jennie was there for a month, slaving in the scullery,

and no whisper came of her release. No replacement was in sight, and Dad in sore need of a mate. But somehow she couldn't get away. Colonel Duncombe wouldn't see her, and she was afraid of the other servants, afraid of the place. It was all so cold and inhuman. Then there was Master Archibald Charles Duncombe, the son and heir. Somehow his very presence in the upper part of the house turned the place into a prison. Of course, the scullery-maid only saw him at a distance, in the care of a nurse, but there was no ignoring his strange, twitching face, the jerking limbs, sudden movements, the queer, high-pitched laughter. Master Archie was fourteen years old, but they daren't let him eat with a knife. It became the stuff of nightmares for Jennie.

Then one evening, with an introduction of hurrying feet and sobbing moans, they brought the night nurse down to the kitchen. Her face was dreadful, gashed and running with blood, hair torn out, and the poor woman sobbing with shock. Master Archie had got hold of the scissors. Fortunately he missed her eyes. She hovered around the kitchen and servants' hall for a day or so, bandaged, swollen and scabby, an object of pity and commiseration. The sense of menace in the upstairs part of the house deepened. How Jennie hated those long, dark, angled corridors and the empty rooms.

Colonel Duncombe put the footman in charge of Master Archie, and increased his wages in consequence. The footman took it all in gloomy resignation, for even to a footman money isn't everything. Only a week or so later, while riding in the trap down to Pocklington, Master Archie seized the whip and beat the footman furiously in the face, cutting him severely. The footman left, indignantly, with his month's wages, and the servants' hall buzzed with fears and rumours. Who would be next?

Jennie really felt she had had enough of Kilnwick Percy. The work, the atmosphere, both above and below stairs, everything was getting her down. She was frightened of every dark corner and corridor as she went about the house. 'I want to go home,' she said to cook. 'He won't let you,' came the automatic reply. 'But I'm only here temporary.' 'He'll never get another maid while you're here.' It was October, over two months in that ghastly house, the nights longer, the darkness surrounding her all the time. It was always dusk in the servants' quarters, and they didn't even get out to go to church.

The new footman, though, was a cheerful, youngish chap, bright-eyed and talkative. It was Jennie's job to fetch milk, butter and eggs from the Home Farm every evening, going up a narrow track through shrubberies gloomy with laurel. That day the servants' hall was talking with dismal relish of the news that young Cess, the farmer's lad, had been seized with religious mania, and was parading up and down the farm track, waving his arms and preaching to imaginary multitudes. Madness seemed to be infectious at Kilnwick, cooped up, yet isolated, as they were.

'I'm not going up there,' said Jennie as she looked out into the threatening dusk. 'You'll have to go,' said cook. 'I'm not going on my own!' The new footman spoke up. 'Do you mind if I go?' 'I don't care who goes, so long as it's company.' So she walked up with the footman, and he was pleasant to talk to, and they didn't meet Cess after all. She rather enjoyed the walk, and went to bed happier that night.

On Monday lunchtime they had the serving hatches open and were laying out food for the servants' hall, and the other servants were gathering, chatting, when suddenly there was a dreadful crash. All the kitchen staff rushed to look. Whatever had happened in the servants' hall to make that havoc? The new footman was lying on the floor! He was rigid, frothing at the mouth, his eyes staring, the end of a long tablecloth clutched in his hand. Plates, glasses and cutlery had scattered round him as he fell. Cook slammed the hatches shut. 'Not another one,' she said. All the other servants crowded out of the hall. What was to be done?'

They waited, listening for sounds, and discussed this new source of amusement for half an hour or so without anyone volunteering to make a move. Then cook said to

Jennie, 'Just go round and look in. You can open the door quietly.' So Jennie went, she was scared, but rather sorry for the footman. She looked in. He was just getting up and seemed quite normal, if rather shaken. So she plucked up the courage to smile in nervous encouragement and stay with him.

'Oh, I'm ever so sorry this has happened,' he said. 'Cook says, would you like a cup o' tea,' Jennie couldn't think of anything else to say. Tea was the great remedy in any emergency. 'Yes, I would.' The footman responded normally and Jennie felt safe to steer him through into the crowded, watchful kitchen. When he was sat down the footman apologized again, 'I'm ever so sorry this has happened, but, you see, I've been out of work, and I think it must be the rich food . . . It's upset me.' He looked round in hangdog appeal. 'I hope nobody'll tell the boss.'

Of course, in a place like Kilnwick it was too much to expect. As soon as the groom picked up Colonel Duncombe at the station he told him. The Colonel sent the footman packing next day. 'He might have fallen with a tray of glasses . . . and broken the lot!' That was how the exchange was reported in the servants' hall.

It was getting on towards Christmas, and this weird behaviour of the new footman, whom she had thought a friend, was the last straw for Jennie. 'I'm going,' she said, and cook as always replied, 'He'll never let you go.' Jennie knew it was true. So, one evening, she packed her bags, got into her travelling clothes and walked out, scared, weary, looking back over her shoulder, almost as if the high, cold house would follow her, with its mad family whipping it on, and swallow her up again.

But she did get away. It was possible to escape, and she reached home two weeks before Christmas. She opened the door and tottered in. Mother looked up, wondering who it might be. Jennie was so thin, tired and pale they didn't know her. Then Mother put her arms round her just as if she were a baby again, and Dad jumped up from his chair. After she had had a good cry and a good comforting, Dad voiced the family reaction to her adventures. 'Well . . . they've made a right mess of thee, haven't they! You ought never to have gone.' With just a glimmer of a smile, followed by a deep sigh, Jennie answered, 'I know that now.'

A letter arrived from Kilnwick Percy just after Christmas. Jennie was reluctant to open it, though she knew she wasn't going back, even if the Colonel himself summoned her. It was from Maggie, and it held some interesting news. 'You ought to have stopped a bit longer, you know, Jennie.' She shuddered at the thought. 'They gave us a pound each to buy a hat, and all the servants were measured for a new dress. Really, I think black quite suits me . . . Even the boss has been better since Master Archie died.'

Never hungered

Christmas Eve and they had only got as far as Goole. Steam tugs, pulling long chains of tom puddings, the iron boxes of coal direct from canal-side mines, had clogged the Aire and Calder Navigation and everyone was behindhand. 'Sleepy Hollow' they called the place, though Dad was philosophical about it, puffed at his pipe and rubbed the peak of his cap thoughtfully as he fixed up a tug to get them to Hull that night. They might, just, deliver their load of sixty tons of washed slack next morning and get home for Christmas dinner. Mother had stayed behind. She was too old for winter life on the keel, and she had never worked the ship much. Jennie didn't mind, she got on well enough with Dad, she was comfortable in her fo'c's'le, and she got a bit more spending money nowadays, as a lass of seventeen should.

'All ready, cap'n.' That was the tug calling Dad. 'Aye.' It was a clear, starlit night, with only a touch of frost, they should have an early sighting of the Whitton lightship and easy passage along the serpentine Humber. Six keels were

going downriver with the ebb tide, in V-formation behind
the tug, three light, three laden. With the tide making up
to three knots they should be in Hull dock by two in the
morning. The lights of Goole sank behind them, and
Jennie could smell the muddy, salt air of the estuary. It
was very still on the Humber, the water moving slowly.

Dad was at the tiller, so she went below for a moment to
make a cup of tea. Dad would take a tot of rum in his. The
cold got right inside you, standing there hour after hour.
Jennie pottered around a bit in the cabin, putting coal on
the fire, folding the table away, sorting out the clutter on
the transom locker. She wasn't that eager to get back on
deck, and there was no need. It promised to be an easy
voyage. After half-an-hour or so, she popped out of the
hatchway with Dad's mug.

Where was he? She couldn't see the mug in her own
hand. It was black dark and fog covered them heavily,
thick as a horse-marine's hide. Not a single star was visible.
The tug was sounding its fog horn and she could hear the
clang of warning bells from the other keels. 'Get on t'bell,'
said Dad, ignoring his tea. They were coming up to the
sandbanks at Whitton, with no prospect of steering by the
lightship. In that shifting channel there was a fair risk of
running aground.

The first shock unbalanced Jennie completely. Hot tea
slopped over her hand and down her skirt. The skirt
wouldn't hurt, but she dropped the mug fast. Hot rum tea
pouring onto her chapped and cracking fingers made her
gasp. The keel lurched half over with the sudden suction
of a mudbank, braking their ninety tons from eight knots
to a violent halt. Jennie tottered backwards, grabbing at
the water barrel. The keel slewed round sideways and a
wave of cold water poured across the decks, soaking her
skirts again. A pause followed when the white world
seemed to spin, silently, in a cocoon of fog. Then came the
second shock, a splintering crash as the vessel behind
drove into their leeboard, shattering its two-inch planking.
It threw Jennie to the deck and the next wave washed right
over her. 'Bloody hell,' yelled Dad, 'the bugger's on top of

us!' Just as Jennie was scrambling to her feet they hit again, driven forwards to collide with the vessel in front, thrusting it right onto the mud. Shaken, wet and frightened, Jennie crawled back to the hatchway and, automatically, closed its cover before she levered herself to her feet.

All was still. The fog wrapped them round so remorselessly that nothing could be seen. The tug engine had stopped. She must be aground as well. They had no time to think about their discomfort. Wet and cold they might be, but only by saving the keel could they save themselves from drowning. Dad took a ten-foot sounding rod and walked round the deck, poking it down into the water. 'Solid all sides,' he said, 'mud and sand . . . We're stuck till morning, that's for sure . . . Aye . . . I reckon it could have been a sight worse, lass . . . Rum's gone, though!' Jennie had to laugh.

Dad went over and tried to make out what the damage to the leeboard might be. They would need those heavy, pear-shaped boards, slung on either side of the vessel like great fins, to hold a course without drifting too much to leeward. Without a leeboard they might well run aground again if they had to make their own way downriver. Mind you, it could be even worse if the weather came on savage and they suffered more damage. Battered to pieces on the mudbank, that would be a fine Christmas. Plenty of folk had drowned in the Humber, and to lose the keel was to lose your livelihood.

You just didn't think of such things. Jennie had faith in her Dad's hard-won wisdom. She was shaking with cold. 'Nowt we can do,' said Dad. 'Let's go below,' and he shoved her towards the hatchway. Jennie made some fresh tea, added rum to both mugs, and they sat in silence, listening to the lap of the water. 'Will the tide float us off, Dad?' Dad was thinking about it. 'Aye, I reckon it might . . . just. But it'll be a close thing. We might need yon tug badly!' He sipped his tea thoughtfully and eased the tight knot in the muffler round his neck. The keel rocked a little, and noises forward, like the clumping of boots, made both of them sit up.

'There's somebody aboard us!' Dad shot up the hatch. He ran across the deck and bumped into two men who had just climbed aboard from a coggy. 'Where are you going?' 'We're going in thy fo'c's'le.' 'What?' 'We're going in t'fo'c's'le. We're not stopping aboard o' that bugger.' One of them pointed out into the fog in the direction of the keel the *Jennie* had driven on to. 'She's going to fill!' Dad knew the captain, and he wasn't with them. 'Well, you're not leaving t'poor old man by himself.' 'We're not stopping aboard there!' Dad argued with them for a while, then came back to the cabin. He couldn't decently deny them the fo'c's'le.

Jennie made more tea. They listened for a while longer. Eventually they heard one of the men get into the boat, row away, and return. More voices, and a deal of cursing, came from the fo'c's'le. 'Th'old man's come now,' said Dad. All three of them were in the fo'c's'le. It would be crowded but safer than where they had been. Jennie settled down to sleep on the cabin lockers as best she could. She was tired enough not to mind hard boards.

Morning was a long time in coming, but at least, when it came, the fog had lifted and they could see the worst. The flood tide had already freed the empty keels. They slipped their ropes and were off downriver. It was Christmas Day, but they might yet fix up a cargo and earn their living. A keelman had to earn his dinner somehow. As they watched, the tug swung clear and began to make its way back up to Goole. They were left to sort things out for themselves. That was the way of the Humber. Jennie made a quick bite of breakfast for the five of them. They would have to wait for high tide whatever happened, either that or shovel out cargo, which meant losing money.

The old captain was looking across at his keel in the grey, morning light. She was heeling far over, driven into the mudbank by the night's collision. He shook his head at the sight. 'She'll fill! Bound to! There's nowt we can do about it . . . she's fixed in yon quicksand.' It was certainly true that she seemed to be going under, with the occasional quiver, like an old pig in the dirt. You could generally expect a keel to right herself, but the suction of the mud was a real danger once it got hold. Dad said, 'If we lift t'hatch corners and shovel coal overboard she may break free.' The others looked doubtful. It wasn't their ship, as *Jennie of Beverley* was Dad's.

'Come on!' They got into both coggy-boats and sculled over. She was heeling so much that her starboard decking was underwater, and they had to begin shovelling out whilst up to their knees in the icy Humber. A little longer and the water would have been in over the hatches and she would have been lost. At least it was easy shovelling out the loose coal at that angle, and, as they shovelled, slowly she began to move, easing out of the mud, righting herself with groanings and the sucking sound of mud letting go. Marvellous to watch, thought Jennie from the deck of their own ship, as her heart warmed to see a worthy keel saved. Dad was pleased with himself when he sculled back, and had another tot of rum to celebrate.

All three vessels were lifted clear by the tide and sailed downriver as the short day was already drawing to a close. They passed the lights of Hessle and Barton and at last saw the glow from Hull docks spreading across the water. They would never get home today, Dad would have to have his Christmas dinner and cigar on Boxing Day. At St Andrew's Dock, where the deep-sea trawlers took on coal, they moored against the wharf. 'I'll do what I can for dinner, Dad,' said Jennie. 'Do you fancy sea-pie?' 'Aye, that'll be grand, love.'

Dad was tired, he couldn't take the long days and sleepless nights as well as when he was a young man. So, while he was making arrangements to deliver the coal next morning Jennie went below to try and conjure up a decent dinner. They had a scrap of beef left in the big brine-pot, so she put it to soak in a bucket of water. Vegetables, a few carrots, leeks and a cabbage, she had bought from a lock-keeper's wife. She made a suet pastry and damped the fire down to a steady, red glow. Cooked in the iron pan on the fire, with a hole in the crust so that the rich, seething gravy ebbed and flowed over it, making the whole a tasty mixture, sea-pie was a favourite dish for both of them when they were tired and cold. It brought you back to life again. At least, on the keels, you never hungered.

A bucket for water

Jennie at eighteen, dressed in her best, with hair pinned up, embroidered skirt, and strong, capable hands, a good chin and a good nose, was the young keelman's dream. She could bake a sea-pie, haul on a rope, scull to shore in all weathers and warm the coldest of bunks. The hard life had developed a wit, sense of humour and self-reliance to carry her through disasters and disappointments. The lads whistled at her when she sailed past and she wasn't above splashing a little canal water absent-mindedly in their direction as a retort, if she had the bucket handy.

One young man they met at Keadby, up the Trent on the way to Sheffield, was particularly taken by a watery introduction, following her with his eyes as she slid, graciously, half-down the hatchway and waited there, posed, talking for a moment to Dad. 'Come on, Jack,' she heard the other ship's captain say. So they called him Jack, did they. Well, it seemed they were to meet Jack everywhere on that trip, following him through the twelve-lock rise at Tinsley and all along the last high level into Sheffield, floating above houses, factories and crowded streets.

Jack began to call regularly at their house when his keel had a cargo to go up the Hull to Driffield. She was invited back to his mother's in Beverley. Jack Porter was his name and Jennie got on very well with him. He was a sensible, pleasant chap. She had lived a working life, mixed with menfolk, knew what to expect of them. She had had other admirers on the keels, but she reckoned Jack Porter would suit very well. One day he might be as good a captain as her Dad. There was no doubt that she could make a good mate for him. So it was agreed, and they were married.

Mother-in-law owned a keel. She had married two keelmen, brothers, one after the other, but had rarely been on the water herself. She was a big, pleasant woman, and Jennie got on with her very well. Jennie and Jack agreed to sail the keel for her and split the profit equally. The keel, *Olive*, was an iron-hulled vessel of one hundred and thirty tons deadweight, with bigger cargo capacity than *Jennie of Beverley*, but needing less maintenance work. Jennie Porter found her a mixed blessing. They had a tiny wash-place, with basin and lavatory, in place of the inevitable bucket, and that was luxury. But, because she was iron, no doors were cut through into the cargo hold from the cabin, so that even when they were travelling home light and moored in heavy rain or fog, thick as a hedge, she still had to carry hot dinners for her husband from the oven in the fo'c's'le, up a vertical ladder, over the hatches and down the ladder into the cabin. And an iron hull was cold, freezing to the touch in winter. She needed that double bunk, Jack's warmth beside her, and, with the folding doors open, the glow from the cabin fire to soothe her to sleep.

Her little boy was born in April 1913, when Jennie was twenty-one. She timed it very well, made sure she was in Beverley for the great event, and was able to carry him on board in his basket for a first summer on the water. They decided to call him Arthur, and he lay in the cabin blowing bubbles happily, staring darkly at the open ventilator above him, soothed by the rocking motion just as Jennie herself had been. Here was another keelman to carry on the line down to the end of the century.

Of course they did have some difficulties. Jennie found she couldn't feed him properly herself and had to manage with powdered baby foods, which were much less convenient. The whole business of heating water, warming bottles and making up the brew at a baby's hours was vexing on a keel. It was downright impossible to lower the sail and feed Arthur at the same time. Breast-feeding would have made life simple. Sometimes he just had to cry. But keel folk had to learn to wait for their meals, bairns or grown men.

August days were hot in an iron-hulled keel, even with both deck-lights unscrewed and replaced with pierced-brass ventilators. Arthur fussed for his drink all the time. They had a built-in sixty-gallon water tank in the side wall above the coal-locker, rather than a barrel on deck as wooden keels had, and it was running low. 'Hoist a bucket, Jennie,' said Jack. They were in Alexandra Dock, so the water lighter came over when it saw the bucket at the masthead and pumped their tank full. Jennie paid her sixpence, grateful for the easy service, and thought no more about it.

Arthur woke them early next morning. Jennie picked him up to come into bed with them, but the lad smelt dreadful. His mess had seeped right through to cover all his clothes, yellow and foul. She warmed a bowl of water and cleaned him up. He was still crying, so she gave him his bottle, rocked him awhile, then laid him down. Arthur was fretful all day, and dirty, from both ends. He didn't seem able to keep anything down. By the time they got to Goole Jennie was worried. They agreed to seek a doctor as soon as they had tied up. The doctor examined Arthur, smelt him and gravely pronounced 'Infantile diarrhoea . . . there's a lot of it about, Mrs Porter.' He didn't seem to think it was very serious. Apparently medicines would only ease Arthur a little, but his body should be able to fight the disease. They would have to wait for Arthur to get better himself. Meanwhile they must boil all the water he drank, which was a nuisance.

They paid the doctor's fee and sailed on. But Arthur got no better. He could keep nothing down, became thinner almost hourly, and fretted day and night. Somehow they managed to get home to Beverley, with a thin, screaming baby, his eyes staring, and Jennie and Jack exhausted with sleepless nights and working days. Arthur died at home in

Beverley, and Jennie vowed to herself she would never have another son.

The war began next year and there were other things to think about than private grief. Keels were in great demand, ferrying coal and iron to make the munitions, foodstuffs to feed the working population, busy day and night, winter and summer. They were given seamen's ration cards, women as well as men, and they needed them. Preparations for war could be seen everywhere, from sandbags piled in the docks to the barrier of old trawlers moored across the mouth of the Humber, to keep out enemy ships or submarines. Jennie and Jack still worked upriver and down, an experienced team.

They had collected one cargo upriver and delivered it to the corn mill in Hull. They had to wait to unload, and spent two sleepless nights listening to the air raid buzzers, waiting for the bombs to fall. The tide was out. *Olive* squatted in the mud as the evening grew darker and buzzers went again. No point in going to bed. 'Let's get out,' said Jack and they climbed up the iron ladder to the roadway on Scott Bridge.

A number of people had gathered to see the fun. The buzzers still sounded. As they watched, a German Zeppelin came upriver, high, shining in the last light, like a shark of the air. Jennie held her breath as it floated by the docks, waiting for the bombs to fall. But it seemed to ignore them, following the Humber upriver into Yorkshire, leaving them still waiting on the ground. Maybe it would be their turn next. 'Bound for Sheffield,' said a man in the crowd. They had heard of some heavy bombing at the munitions factories in Sheffield, and a lot of deaths. Jennie shivered. 'Are t'cold, missis?' 'Nay, I'm frightened.'

The all clear sounded. They made their way back to *Olive* and tried to sleep. Next morning a ship's husband came up to them. 'Dost' want a job, Jack?' 'I do! Anything as long as I get clear of Hull!' 'We've a cargo of nuts wants fetching from Keadby. Reckitts want it right away.' 'I'll go anywhere as long as I can get clear of Hull . . . and get a good night's sleep!'

They fixed up a tug right away, and by evening were snugly moored half-way up the Trent. In open country, far from any military target, they could sleep free of fear. Jennie made a quick dinner, then they went straight to bed and to sleep. The waking was terrifying. A great, reverberating boom, like a giant drum-note, as something struck and shook the empty keel. The clock, sugar basin, all the pots, fell to the floor. Jennie and Jack jumped end over in bed, struggling to get out of the bedclothes. *Olive* was still rocking fiercely. 'Good God!' yelled Jack, 'it's a bloody submarine!'

He shot up the hatch in his shirt. Jennie could just see his white calves in the universal darkness as she tried to follow. No explosions, no fire, not even a Zeppelin above them, as they burst out on deck. Then from a black shape just downriver, came an apologetic voice. 'I don't think we've hurt thee, Jack.' It was the captain of another iron keel that had been coming fast with the ebb and run into them. 'No,' Jack shouted back, once the facts had sunk into his sleep-dazed brain, 'but you've bloody well frightened us to death!'

They really had very few problems with submarines in the estuary during the war. Life was more difficult, rather than dangerous. They used to stock up with meat in Hull before going on a trip, buying a side of bacon or a ham to put in the brine-pot, but now meat was rationed, and not always to be had. Jack generally did the shopping, and always came back grumbling. So, one day, when they were moored in Alexandra Dock, he sent Jennie. 'No, you go for a change!'

Outside the dock there was a pork butcher's on one side and a shop selling beef on the other, with long queues by both of them. 'It'll take a hour or two to get through,' thought Jennie when she saw the queues, 'and we can't wait for tug or tide.' She decided to look in the beef window. The fish-shed women, who worked nearby and formed most of the queue, turned to stare at her. They were a rough lot. What was she up to? 'Now, missis! What do you want?' It was a policeman. 'Well, I was just wondering . . . If I've got to wait behind all these folk, we'll never get t'ship off.' 'Where are you going?' 'To Goole at dinner time.' 'Have you got seaman's rations?' 'Yes.' She showed him the card. 'All right,' he looked at the queue, 'I'll see you in.'

She could feel the wave of anger that ran after her into the shop. She heard the comments about queue-jumping when she came out, saw the stony, threatening faces. Jennie hurried back to Jack, shaking. 'You should just hear them folk,' she said, 'I'm not going for no meat no more!' Jack laughed at her, but Jennie was serious. 'It's a man's job that . . . I'd sooner lower sail in a storm any day!'

Time and the war had buried her early grief over losing Arthur. There were some other matters that disturbed a woman's nights in the cabin besides Zeppelins and submarines. You couldn't be careful all your life, not with a husband about. As soon as she knew she was pregnant, though it was four years since Arthur's death, Jennie knew this one was going to be a girl. She dreamed of having a pretty little girl, a little angel in frocks and curls.

Jennie stayed at home to have the baby. It was still war time, but Beverley was always a peaceful place, and there were no complications. This baby seemed quite happy to come into the world. 'There now,' said the midwife, 'it's a lovely little boy, Mrs Porter.' Jennie really didn't hear it for she was rather tired. She reached out for her little girl, and when the close-wrapped baby with its fine, fair hair, was put in her arms for the first time, she held it close and fell asleep. It took her a while to realize there had been a mistake, though she saw the evidence every time she changed the baby. She loved to dress him up in frocks and would sit, stitching at smocking for him in the evenings. 'He's like a little doll,' said her sister-in-law, cuddling him, and Jennie would smile in satisfaction. He wasn't going to be a boy like the last one, even if he couldn't be a girl.

The baby soon settled in to life on the keel. She always boiled his water and he was no trouble. When he started to crawl they fixed a line to him so that he was safe to explore round the deck. In rough weather Jack sat him in a zinc-plated tub on deck, lashed to a stanchion, and, as the keel rolled sides-under so that the waves washed his tub from side to side, little Jack would crow with laughter. Pretty baby or not, little Jack was beginning life as a keelman.

Jennie kept him pretty for as long as she could, until her husband took to saying, 'When are t'going to breech that lad?' She knew she had to do it, but it meant the end of the lass she had longed for. She loved making the dresses, and he had such a delicate face to go with them. But she knew 'get that lad breeched', would echo through her nights until the proper, male, thing was done. Only when he was a year old could she bring herself to agree to it. So they called on some relatives in Sheffield, and had him shortened there. The ceremony didn't take long, the fair curls soon fell under the scissors, but it was like losing a daughter again.

Jennie worked so hard at keeping everything clean that they christened *Olive*, 'the washing ship'. Even when they were on the way back from Sheffield after that sad shortening, and little Jack was no longer in frocks and curls, the flags of laundry hung everywhere on stays and lines. 'By gum, Jennie,' said a bank ranger, as he stared at the display, 'I were allus a bonny bairn . . . but I'd never as many slips as that!' She could have hit him.

Hauling in

Parkhill colliery, near Wakefield, had a washing place for keelmen, with scrubbed white tables, coppers of hot water and room to move. Jennie took full advantage of it after they had loaded, to clean up herself and young Jack. At five years old he was no longer the same little angel, though a good lad enough. *Olive* was ready to sail as soon as the ablutions were over, so Jennie started feeling comfortable and clean. Shortly after Castleford and the junction with the Aire and Calder canal, they met a head wind and slowed to a stop. 'Get on t'hatches,' shouted Jack, 'pull t'sail in.'

Jennie jumped to it. Rollers, like a horizontal capstan, with slots for the handle, carried ropes that ran to the masthead and supported the main yard. Because keels were square-rigged, both yard and sail must be swung down and under the mast stays when they were lowered to lie fore and aft. It was rather a tricky job in a stiff wind, but Jennie had been doing it for twenty years and she knew just how to manoeuvre the heavy, canvas bundle so that it settled evenly on the hatches rather than dropping over the side.

Jack was at the rollers. 'All right?' 'All right.' He let it drop. Jennie grabbed at the yard as it swung sideways. She felt the canvas in her hands. Then she was falling backwards over the edge as the weight of the thing caught her unexpectedly. Through the air she went, skirts ballooning, and into the water. 'I just clicked hold on t'rope,' she says, 'or I'd've been away.' Hanging by one hand, she looked up despairingly at her family, and saw young Jack, her little angel, in roars of laughter at his mother's acrobatics. At this she found her voice, and her indignation. 'Come here! . . . both of you . . . and pull me out!' They were quick enough when it was needed, but young Jack was still chuckling, and she could see a suppressed grin on old Jack's face as they hauled their dripping bundle out of the canal. Jennie's dignity wouldn't let her say anything else once she was safe, so she went below to change in silence, rather hurt by her son's laughter. It was just like a man.

'Right,' said her husband when she was back on deck, 'we'd best take t'mast down as well. Tha can come over to t'fore-rollers wi' me.' He looked her seriously in the face, but she could tell he might laugh at any minute. What could she say? It was even beginning to seem a little funny to her, in retrospect. Jack pulled the bar out of the lutchet, the mast socket, and they wound the mast down, carefully, to rest on the hatches. Next thing, she knew, she would be on the bank, hauling.

They did have some fun and games on board, particularly now the great war was over, and work not as pressing. It was hot one August, in the 1920s and life on the water was tempting for its appearance of coolness. They had a cargo of cement to take from Earl's cement works in Hull to Leeds. Jack's mother was in the house when the bargain was struck. 'I'd like to go to Leeds,' she said. 'You have to get up early, you know.' 'Well, I don't mind. I'd like to go to Leeds.' 'Of course you can come, if you like.' 'Aye', said Jack, 'we'll be leaving Earl's at four o'clock tomorrow morning.'

'Your mother won't come,' said Jennie when they were on the river, 'she couldn't sleep in t'fo'c'sle bed, she's too big.' 'Well, I don't know,' Jack replied, 'she's game, is mother, I reckon she might sleep on t'bags of cement.' 'Oh, I don't mind thy mother.'

They spent the day loading up and went to bed at dark. Four o'clock next morning, as they were getting ready, Jack's mother appeared on the bankside, like a large, floral sack in her print dress, with a coat over it and a case in her hand. Jennie rowed over to pick her up.

Mother-in-law settled in very well, but they knew she wasn't used to the life. Next morning they would have a tug from Hull harbour at three. 'You needn't get up, mother.' 'Oh, I'll get up. I'm going to see all there is to see.' Jennie groaned inwardly, her mother-in-law was certainly game, but she fairly took up space in the cabin and she always stood in the way when they were working the boat. But they were towed up the Humber in flat, pearly, morning light and mother-in-law enjoyed every minute of it. Young Jack told her what to look for and it kept them both out of mischief.

Goole by seven o'clock, and time to shop in the market. Then they continued up-river. The lad and his grandma sat with their feet in the water to cool off as the day grew hotter. 'How much further is it?' she kept asking, 'By, it's a long way.' 'We're not nearly there yet.' They had lunch, just bread and cheese, then tea, on deck. Jack moored for half-an-hour while Jennie cooked dinner. After midnight they reached Leeds lock. 'Well, I didn't think you had days as long as this,' said mother-in-law as her eyes blinked drowsily. Leeds Town Hall clock was striking one, they could hear it clearly across a silent, sleeping city.

They laid *Olive* up against the wharf, ready to unload, and went to bed. At six o'clock banging on the deck rousted them out. It was time to deliver the cargo. Mother-in-law sat on the deck, owlishly sleepy, idly watching the work. 'Ooh . . . come and look here, Jennie.' 'What's t'matter?' Jennie had her work to do, she couldn't just be a spectator. 'Oooh, come and look. I've never seen nowt like this.' 'What is it then?'

Jennie eventually found a moment to go over to the fore-end, where her mother-in-law was staring across the wharf. What was it all about? Two lasses, apparently, who were washing at a drinking fountain let into the wall, stripped to the waist, their breasts hanging, water dripping from their nipples. Mother-in-law looked amazed at this picture of low life. 'Nay,' Jennie, the experienced traveller told her, 'it's regular is that,' and went back to work. There were plenty of street walkers in Leeds. She'd seen them before.

Mother-in-law always talked afterwards about her adventures on the keel. She was a kind-hearted woman and helpful with domestic arrangements when they were called away. Jennie normally did the baking on Sunday mornings to have bread ready for the week. The fo'c's'le oven was too small for decent-sized loaves, and if they were short of bread on a voyage she used to bake bread-cakes. That Sunday Jack had gone out for a 'keelman's honeymoon,' a walk along the beck to the river-lock and back again, just to see how things were with the keels. Jennie's baking bowl was full of dough, dinner was in the oven and they were settled for a full day at home, when she heard a knock at the door.

'Oh it's you,' said Jennie, recognizing a ship's husband from Hull. 'I want you in dock for next morning, Jennie.'

'Well, t'keel's at Leven!' The short Leven canal turned off the river Hull north of Beverley, so they would have to go and get *Olive* and then bring her downriver to Hull if they wanted this job. 'Oh well, he'll have to get her then. I can't wait.' The man was off. Jennie sighed, looking at her dough. But you couldn't afford to turn down a cargo.

Shortly afterwards Jack came in. Jennie eyed him grimly. 'We're to be in dock for t'morning . . . what are we going to do?' 'Oh . . . we shall have to go to Leven.' 'Well, I've a bowl o'bread. What'll I do wi' it?' Jack took this in his stride. 'We'll fetch our Olive!' That was Jack's sister who, following tradition, had the same name as the keel. 'Let her bake it. Just put it in tins, ready.' 'And how am I going to get to Leven?' 'You can go on Olive's bike.'

Jack went along the street to his mother's and she came back right away with him. 'It's all right, Jennie. You put t'bread in t'oven and I'll see to it.' So Jennie packed up some lunch and set off with Jack on the bike to collect the keel. They reached her while it was still light, but the wind was unhelpful, and Jack said they must haul her. 'We've got to be in Hull in t'morning.'

Jennie was on the bank. She buckled the seal, a leather harness like a cart-horse wore, round her and clipped the main-line to it. Then she leaned into the harness, feeling *Olive*'s weight. The worst bit was getting under way, getting all those tons moving, when your guts heaved at every step. 'I just hope it's not to Hull . . . right to Hull . . . down to Hull,' she said to herself with every heaving step. She'd done it before, but it left her tired to death next day. You could pull your insides out with a keel. Thank God they didn't have a cargo on board.

The evening was drawing in. She had to move fast when bushes loomed up out of the canal mist and threatened to tangle the line. She couldn't afford to stop and take time to free it. *Olive* was under way and would just drag her in as she went. Another bush! No, a damned cow on the bank. It lurched off into the misty water meadows at the last minute. That would be real fun and games, if she tangled with a cow.

Jennie had settled into her stride, a steady, walking pace which was quite comfortable when the keel was light. But something else was moving in the mist ahead, perhaps another cow? No, it was two people, a courting couple. They made room for her. She plodded past them, a woman in her thirties, hauling this great barge, and they said nothing. But, as Jack drew abreast, standing at the tiller, the girl shouted at him. 'Tha great, big, fat devil. Tha wants to be on that bank, never mind that woman!' Jack was quiet for a minute, then he chuckled. Folk on land would never understand. Soon afterwards they moored for the night.

Next morning they had an ebb-tide down to Hull, and a fair wind at the lock. They set sail in confidence that they would reach Hull in time. As they came past the end of Beverley Beck Jennie could see mother-in-law waving from the bank. Jack steered closer. 'It's all right, Jennie,' she called, through cupped hands, 'bread's all right . . . Olive's took it out.' And that was that.

The next war came when Jennie was nearing fifty. She felt tired by it all, as if she had seen it all before. Just as in 1914, so in 1939, they had more heavy cargoes to deliver under difficult conditions. Because of the bombers they had to work without lights, even in winter. One day in the second year of the war, they were coming upriver from Hull, hoping to get home, to light a fire and have a rest after a long time away. It was March, freezing cold, and by the time they got to Sutton bridge, black, dark, nearing midnight. They had gone on too long. They wouldn't get home that day. It was time to find moorings.

'Get in t'boat,' said Jack, 'take the line.' Jennie lumbered into the coggy-boat with the half-anchor in one hand. She was tired, frozen through, wrapped up in a coat, muffler, woollen headscarf and thick gloves. She couldn't feel her fingers, but she knew they were split with frost and the ends rubbed raw on sailcloth and ropes. My, they wouldn't half sting when she got to bed and they thawed out.

'I'll shove thee off,' was Jack's next instruction, 'when t'boat hits t'bank – jump!' She crouched down, could see nothing in front, felt the shock as they touched, and jumped blind. No bank, nothingness for a moment, then Jennie was in the freezing water. Right under she went, feeling it hit her face like a blow and begin to soak through her clothes. She yelled at the shock. The boat drifted away. She clung to the bank and yelled again. *Olive* was away down the canal.

Jennie grabbed onto a tuft of grass and tried to make herself move. She was so tired, her clothes soaking and heavy. She could hardly feel her legs anymore. Then she heard voices. 'Are you all right, missis?' Jennie shook her head. 'Are you all right?' The shouting came to her muffled ears more clearly. 'I don't know,' she mumbled. Jennie was crying with cold now, but the words got her moving. Somehow she forced energy into her numb, tired body and managed to crawl out onto the bank, slithering and gasping like a stranded fish.

She was sobbing with cold, her boots full of water, soaked clothes clinging to her in wet heaviness. *Olive* was nowhere to be seen. It was wartime, pitch black, no flashlights permitted. Jennie began a stumbling run along the bank that seemed to be taking her nowhere and to go on forever. It might have been a mile or so, how could she tell? She simply shuffled mechanically forwards until a blacker mass in the surrounding blackness loomed in front of her. She grunted. A voice answered. 'Jennie?' 'Aye.' 'Not drowned then.' 'No.' 'Right, we'll have to turn her round . . . Get ready.'

But that night was proving too much even for the stalwart Jennie Porter. 'You can do what you like,' she answered through chattering teeth. 'Send me yon boat! I'm coming aboard to get these wet things off!' Jack left attending to *Olive* for a moment, pushed the coggy-boat over with a stower and helped her on board.

Jennie did the most sensible thing she could think of. Stripping completely on deck, she shot down to the cabin, wrapped herself in a blanket, poured out a glass of port-wine and topped it up with hot water from the kettle. Then she got into bed and drank it, leaving Jack to moor. Thank

God it was over. She closed her eyes and felt the throbbing in her fingers.

Jack shoved her again. 'Get up! Get up . . . there's summat up. Hurry!' Jennie groaned as she turned sideways. Surely she had only just got to sleep. She seemed to be wedged in the corner with Jack sitting almost on top of her, struggling with the clothes. 'What time is it?' she asked. 'I don't know – three o'clock maybe!' 'Three in the morning!' Jack was out of the bunk, but leaning over her at a peculiar angle, trying to light the oil-lamp. 'Come on,' he said, 'we're on a pile-end.' That was it. That was why the floor was sloping. The rim around the hull, which looked like the rolled edge on a tin can, must have wedged on a pile, and now the tide had gone down, leaving them tipped up in the air. They might heel completely over . . . and after such a night.

Jennie pulled on some dry clothes and followed him on deck. It was foggy now, the fog freezing on all the ropes and fittings. Nothing to see except a cocoon of fog. 'Get into that boat,' said Jack. 'Not likely! No . . . I've had enough of that tonight. You're not getting me in that boat no more.' 'Come on Jennie – we've got to haul her off.' 'If you want to take a line over, then you'll have to get in t'boat yourself.'

So Jack took the end of the wire rope across the canal in the little boat and fixed it securely round a tree. Then they both began to haul on the roller handles. *Olive* was leaning steeply over. They couldn't risk having the cargo shift in the hold, or she would turn over and they might well go under with her.

She didn't want to move. Just sat there like a solid ingot of iron, stubborn and heavy. 'Heave,' said Jack as they tried again, and Jennie heaved at the handle, aching with the effort. The rope snapped. Resistance suddenly ceased. Both of them fell to the deck, Jennie quite desperate now to have it all over and go back to bed. Jack rowed back to fix the rope again. Heaving in a stupefied exhaustion, at last they felt her moving slowly, reluctantly, off the pile until she gradually slid clear.

They both came back to the cabin. Jack looked at the kettle meaningfully. He obviously needed a cup of tea. But Jennie was in no mood for ordinary comforts. 'That's t'finish,' she said as she began to climb into bed. 'No more winters aboard this keel!' Jack made to speak but she ignored him. 'You can do what you like . . . I'll go out charring afore I'll do this again!' It was a desperate threat, but she turned her face to the wall, refusing to say any more, and seething with such anger that Jack had begun to snore before exhaustion took over and she fell asleep.

In the morning it was still bitterly cold, but they had an easy run up to Beverley. They didn't say much about the night's happenings until Jack tried to dismiss the subject lightly. 'Oh, you'll be all right . . . You'll forget it.' Then she turned on him. 'I'll never forget last night . . . not as long as I live!' Jennie remained adamant. No more winters aboard, and that was that. Mother-in-law came round to try and make things more comfortable. 'Oh, Jennie'll forget it,' she said, and Jennie blazed up again. 'Don't you think so for a minute!'

The summer of 1941 was pleasant on the keel, but Jennie didn't change her mind. They sailed regularly through Goole on a coal contract for Grovehill Shipyard. Jack knew a ship's husband who worked out of Goole, and on one trip he spoke to him at the lockhead. 'Does thy boss want a keel, Walter?' 'Why? What for? Are t'thinking of selling out?' 'Aye . . . Jennie says she won't have another winter aboard. I can't carry on on my own . . . I want to sell her.' 'Oh well, I'll see my boss.'

Jennie didn't feel she could make any remarks about this conversation, and she wasn't really expecting it to come to anything. When they sailed back to Keadby and the Trent, missing out Goole, she thought to herself 'that's goodbye to selling *Olive*.'

They were at home in Beverley next Monday, the washing was on the line and she and Jack had just sat down to dinner, when there was a knock at the door. 'Go and see who it is.' 'No, I aren't going. You go.' So she sighed and went. 'No thank you, not today.' He was a ragged-looking man in leggings. 'Is this Mr Porter's?' he asked. Jennie looked at him again. 'Yes.' 'Can I have a word with him? . . . I've come about *Olive*.' 'Oh,' said Jennie, and smiled. 'Come in, do!'

Jack was already at the table. 'Have you had your dinner?' she asked the man. 'No, I came straight up from Goole after Walter told me.' 'Well, have a bite with us.' So they had some dinner, and then, while Jennie was clearing up the plates he turned to Jack. 'I hear you want to sell *Olive*, then?' 'Yes, I do.' Jennie was careful not to rattle the cutlery as she washed up. 'Can we have a talk about what you want for her?' 'All right, let's walk down and have a look.' Just like a man, to march off and bargain away in private, leaving her to wait anxiously at the sink.

Young Jack came back from work at tea-time. She told him, briefly, what was afoot. 'Your Dad'll never sell *Olive*,' she said, knowing how it had always been his life. At last Jack came in. The man from Goole wasn't with him. She waited, looking at his face. He didn't seem either glad or sorry. 'Well, it's done!' 'What! Have you selled it?' 'Aye.' 'Thank God for that.' And they sat down to tea.

All Futura Books are available at your bookshop or newsagent, or can be ordered from the following address:
Futura Books, Cash Sales Department,
P.O. Box 11, Falmouth, Cornwall.

Please send cheque or postal order (no currency), and allow 45p for postage and packing for the first book plus 20p for the second book and 14p for each additiona book ordered up to a maximum charge of £1.63 in U.

Customers in Eire and B.F.P.O. please allow 45p for the first book, 20p for the second book plus 14p per copy for the next 7 books, thereafter 8p per book.

Overseas customers please allow 75p for postage an packing for the first book and 21p per copy for each additional book.